GOTHIC ROCK BLACK BOOK

MICK MERCER

"Moderation is a fatal thing, Lady Hunstanton.
Nothing succeeds like *excess*."

(Oscar Wilde)

"So who's this Lady Hunstanton geezer?"

(Mick Mercer)

ACKNOWLEDGEMENTS

Mawkish, blushing, simpering, intuitively vibrant and positively draining thanks are extended to the following, who have made the passing of this book just that little bit easier;
All hacks/hackettes who breathlessly find their work saddled with my company, Dylan Thomas (unwittingly), Chris Charlesworth, Karen Holmes and Karen Ehlers, Gordon Slag, Paul Wright, Steve Brown, various fanzines . . . and Mat Smith, without whom . . . the world would be a less degenerate place.

© Copyright 1988 Omnibus Press
(A Division of Book Sales Limited)
Edited by Chris Charlesworth

Book Designed by Laurence Bradbury/Sarah Collins
Picture Research by Mary McCartney
Project and typesetting co-ordinated by Caroline Watson

ISBN 0.7119.1546.6
Order No. OP44866

All rights reserved. No part of this book may be reproduced in any form or by any electronic or mechanical means, including information storage or retrieval systems, without permission in writing from the publisher, except by a reviewer who may quote brief passages.

Exclusive distributors:

Book Sales Limited
8/9 Frith Street,
London W1V 5TZ, UK

Music Sales Corporation
225 Park Avenue South,
New York, NY 10003, USA

Music Sales Pty Limited
120 Rothschild Avenue,
Rosebery, NSW 2018, Australia

To the Music Trade only:
Music Sales Limited,
8/9 Frith Street,
London W1V 5TZ, UK

Picture credits:

PETER ANDERSON p67 Back Cover (TR). ERICA ECHENBERG p18/19. JOAN GEOFFROY p62 (T&C) 69. JAYNE HOUGHTON p20 (R) 68 (T). LONDON FEATURES INT. p5 6/7 8 (T&B) 9 (T&B) 11 12/13 20 (L) 24/25 41 50 (T&B) 55 61 63 74 93 Back Cover (TL&C). ACTION PACT p58. JARED PEPALL p72/73 79. LINDA ROWELL p21 59. TOM SHEEHAN p10 14 15 24 (T&C&B) 26 27 29 30 33 34/35 37 38/39 40 43 44/45 46 47 48/49 51 53 60 64/65 71 76/77 81 84/85 86 88/89 90/91 94/95 Back Cover (BL&R).

Every effort has been made to trace the copyright holders of the photographs in this book but one or two were unreachable. We would be grateful if the photographers concerned would contact us.

Typeset by Capital Setters, London.
Printed in England by Courier International Ltd, Tiptree, Esse

CONTENTS

GOTH'S SPECKLED HISTORY: PART ONE
1966 AND ALL THAT

To begin in the middle. It is Winter, discontented, and a guileful night, full of guilt, heavy with indiscretion. The pavements resound to the clunking, silver-shod feet of the bible-black, the throwback, slow black, crowblack, swept back, slung-back, get back, go back, Edgar Allen Poeblack, feathered hairskrees that leave subterraneans left for dead. Quite simply it's raining bats and Gods. You've guessed it, they're Goths all right.

The Goths are a happy, obnoxious, querulous, perilous crowd that few adrift from their bitter glow care to consider and even more prefer to dismiss as antique road shows. This is peevish night blindness and outright shallow stupidity on the part of the observer for the Goths are the last current bastion of life as a physical work of art, are the last seething mass of addled optimism and the last people you want on the Tube with you late at night after a Mission concert. (The *noise!*)

They, as much as their music, are a cruelly maligned breed. Sometimes, given a seemingly forced propensity for errant stupidity you can but throw back your head and . . . hope that somebody catches it — because someone deserves to *catch it*, considering rock's recent intrusion into a once steaming arena of sizzling sensuality and frozen smiles — as the travelling, unravelling brains of Goth devotees does strain the patience, as your average (generally exceedingly average) indie fan blushes to their roots and slips another weedily embarrassing tome into their carrier bags. Goths really *are* the Great Plague, the Black Death of cynicism, who have grown and spread while all around cry cultural starvation. This book simply takes a peek.

If you are confused by Goth and its nascent appeal, then so you jolly well should be, old bean! It is an instinctive blend of the possible and the strictly unlikely, even the unlikeable, a marriage made in Hell but with a few well appointed skylights thrown in. A hotbed therefore of hilarity, mountainous pretensions, leviathan characters and undying passion. At its heart there is little or nothing, but in its head *everything*. This you have to come to terms with totally or not at all.

Unlike many miniaturised scenes today which are merely generic imposters of their predecessors, Goth invented *itself* and has continued to grow like a misshapen old bear, with the historical allegations often hard to justify. Calling it 'Goth', except when the word is used with clinical correctness, is a monstrous abuse of a proud, if blind, beast, as brave as poking your tongue out at Stevie Wonder. Regardless of public opinion, where it is generally disregarded as an opiate, Goth just retreats into its shell and ruptures beautifully, ready for the next stage. Having grown progressively more popular, as proved by the weakened, lightened chart formation teams, as, in some cases, exhibited here, it has conversely become more abrasive and threatening on the underground, and continues to flourish because it has no rules. The one sea grave expressly designated for loners.

Think back to Punk, and ignore the smell. It took only three years to burn out, be molested by knaves and reinstated with pop to leave only the toilet-sniffers and dreg ends of politico-punk left on the streets. Goth has been thriving and striving for at least *seven* crisp years and only recently recognised as a movement.

The Cult — Little darlings, every one of them

4

WOLF CO...

Pretty slow movement by anyone's standards, yet still with room for massive extensions and improvement. Kinda spooky, huh? Less mundane than the usual mainstream, indie alternatives, with a vicious kick for its beat, Goth sounds as attractive when wounded and bleeding as when healthy and chubby. Goth is a state of mind. And what a *state* some of the minds are in. Witchcraft entanglement, for the very dense, has recently caused concern in the Church of England, and that's official! Anything can happen during Goth's peak time, and that's outside office hours! It goes, considering trajectory, from the well intentioned pop of All About Eve to the pompous but powerful rock of The Cult to the audacious adrenalin omelettes of Sisters Of Mercy, and that's only the basics.

At grass-roots level, although it would be cuter to say that *no grass grows*, the conversely twisted bands are harder-edged than before, opting for self-immolation and verbal degradation, and anyone who prefers to lick the surface and limply pronounce Goth as *merely* a new rock movement would be well advised to steer clear of smaller events. It wouldn't blow their credibility, but their noses would be out of joint, permanently. (It is not advisable to laugh at a Goth.)

Goth, as a world within a world within a *whirl*, can truthfully be traced only as far back as the rise of Bauhaus, when their image and scabrous sound enveloped the dingy gig circuit. Their importance, or impotence, depending on your stance (hands on hips, nose distinctly uppish), *is* obvious and far more so than any oblique references to the late sixties/ early seventies. Those particular influences are there *by association*, as performer's

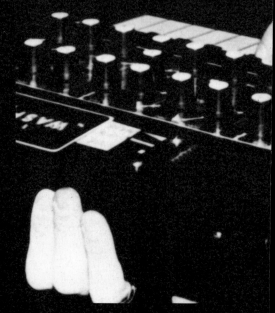

Peter Murphy — with the revamped stylophone that never took off.

influences come to bear, but not as a direct catalyst in the first place. If we're considering the stream of consciousness as much as a stream of dbarma bum's diarrhoea, then it can be said that Patti Smith plays as much a part in verbal venality as those torpid tones of Jim Morrison.

If Rock is now, in the ways of the wasteful, the byword for the most creative forces in Goth, as opposed to easiest to assimilate, then you can look back in wonder at the slack symbolism of Black Sabbath, the intolerable elegance of Led Zeppelin and even the likes of Steppenwolf and Blue Oyster Cult for an easily picked pocket of moves. The lie of the land has tilted with an influx of heavy metal aficionados, who kept their skeletons firmly locked away three years ago, but as yet has done little in the way of producing truly momentous moments, managing instead a subtle, at best, merging of the elements, updating the sounds of the sixties and seventies, but *stifling* the eighties. No doubt all this will turn around in two years' time and Pop will be the overriding factor of fashionability. It is all as relevant as anything else after all. Goth is there to be abused. A sadist's delight on a Winter's night, as the ravens *squat* the Tower.

The weakly magic(k)al imagery of the past had to make itself felt in Goth, and was always bound to be absorbed, just as the guitar sound, based upon 'heroes', hangs like smoke in the angst-ridden ambience of darkness, where a couple of years ago most people were turning their ears inside out with the spindly sound of The Velvet Underground, and the power, hopelessly implanted into some bands, of the MC5 or The Stooges. Some things are better left untouched, like hedgehogs in

Far left top: Jim Morrison. Unconscious guru. Missing, presumed dead.

Far left bottom: Patti Smith, looking vaguely like a member of Pop Will Eat Itself. Her impact was immense, her output less so.

Left: Black Sabbath. "We don't need no steenkin' haircuts."

Below: Led Zep. On the original stairway to Heaven. What punk regarded as a total waste of airspace, Goth has since rehabilitated.

the road. The Mission could almost *be* the 'Barnstorm' album that made Joe Walsh's name, simply spring-cleaned, but it really doesn't matter because you can moan at Goth as much as muzzle up against it. There is so much room in this malicious mansion that one, personally subjective, closed toilet does not warrant a hail of invective. All of the main bands have their faults, all have their moments of glory. It really doesn't matter who beats who, who hates who. Hatred is another word for wasted time and corrupted energy.

Originally, when Goth's musky flavour was virtually the only antagonistic thing around *to* savour, at the start of the Eighties, people were too content being forward thinking, nose deep in the truffle search for excitement, and the only past imagery they accepted were ludicrously

Siouxsie And The Banshees. Modern Goth started here. (Much to their disgust.)

blurred glimpses of The Damned's Dave Vanian with his vampiric obsessions, although this was a one-way joke only, as their music didn't back it up, and some remarkable Siouxsie shots, inevitably called Queen Goth, which even Giger couldn't have matched. The Banshees it was who, a few years later, would inadvertently produce the Bert Weedon 'Play Goth In A Day (or your nightmares back)' book, in the lazy trails of 'Arabian Nights'. It is virtually a blueprint for the more pliable Goth bands, with its metriculous bass and shuffling drum patterns, its circling guitar and its spirited cacophony of vocals that dart out of gentle warmth. If you haven't played it in years then dig it out pronto, and cackle, if you must.

Goth is more than a futile wheeze, it is a quiet, still world, often thoughtful, with a neat line in abruptly consumptive gigs, where poetry and poetic intentions are wrested back from the sneering intellectual and all pedestals aerated, where emotions are rarely given sharp clarity as they are there to produce a smokescreen for the listener to hide inside.

We shall of course call it Goth, even though you could just consider it a violently childish dreamworld, involving immense amounts of energy *and* play-acting. A Goth gig, at its best, is like a banquet, while a typical indie evening is a spoon lodged in the small intestine of life. That fact is undeniable. What Goth usually lacks is the supreme *starburst* of something truly musically engaging — Sugarcubes, Big Black, Pixies, Soho, the list again depends on personal preferences but you'll have no doubt caught the drift — because its own music is usually too leaden, whereupon the

social element comes into play. You don't *need* the band *per se*. The evening is entertainment enough. That doesn't happen elsewhere, outside of clubs. As I write there are similar tendencies and rites enacted nightly within the skate and hardcore fraternity, celebrating the rebirth of an abortion, but that will dwindle and die, just as before. Goth, for reasons of taste, tact and terror, survives.

Wracked with religious imagery, slippy with sexual inference, Goth onstage is rarely happy. Goth offstage is a hoot. Goth onstage cries, growls and scowls. Goth offstage goes quietly insane and wraps itself in drunken worship, pagan worship, and the loins of psychologically damaged French philosophers; its history measured in centuries rather than trivial 'youth' generations. Led Zeppelin, or Baudelaire? The choice isn't *too* difficult. Or shouldn't be.

And hey kids, I was there, lurking in the corners and nibbling my pencil! From Siouxsie's constipated grace, grabbed and shaken, *literally*, by Pete Murphy, before any of us knew he was a big softie, bemused by Southern Death Cult, soothed by Danse Society, intrigued by Sex Gang, whipped senseless by

Siouxsie. Ice queen to ice cream.

Belfegore, knocked sideways by Nephilim's guttural roar, enticed by the sweet gyrations of All About Eve's grip on reality, annoyed by Bible For Dogs or simply shocked by Sleeping Dogs Wake. Can't fool me.

This book doesn't pay homage, it doesn't extend a whitewashing hand, because criticism of Goth has too long panted in a void of ignorance and fluffy drivel. Frivolity has a major role to play, as only a fool loves *everything*.

So ignore the historical aspect that strays too far from a purely believable path. Goth, unlike punk, already has extensive international support, throughout Europe and America and especially in Japan, almost from the word go. (Countries with hot climates funnily enough view it with total disinterest.) In this septic isle, where it holds the higher position, it does *mean* something, it does *need* to be scrutinised without excessive approval.

Its black flag is a flag of cynicism for all to follow, for their own motives, with their own motifs, in the cause of paralysing withdrawal symptoms. In its own weird way it is even quite rarefied, being the main non-instrumental form of music to act as 'mood music', where you lay your own thoughts into place, disregarding any lyrics which might come your way. In this way Christian Death, a criminally underrated band, with labels in at least seven countries, are forerunners of gloomy classical soirées, and so successful that they actually have to turn down some majors' offers because it would lose them money.

Goth will die, but only when there are sufficient bands of strength around who do not belong to any one movement. So far we have had shambling, jangling,

jingling, hippy, grebo, indie-pop, cutie-pop, anorak-pop and speed/skate/thrash metal since Goth beamed into view, and none of them have, or will, last half as long. There is an indication that independence of thought is growing and perhaps in three years Goth will slip away quietly in our sleep. It implants by its very weariness cancer cells in the valve. It takes a lot of explaining, but very little understanding to see that Goth is an invisible substance at the heart of empathic but essentially differing *forms*

Dave Vanian and Vampire Chic. (Well, he's got the teeth for it.)

of music – Goth in reality being its audience – and when those forms become larger it takes people away and impetus shrivels. Until then remember the words of Nostradamus when he said, did he not, 'and there will come an Eldritch whose nose looks mightily odd at times'. And right now consider the suitably imaginative definition that my dictionary revealed:-

GOTH-IC. *adj. Abbr.* Goth. 1. a. Of or pertaining to the Goths and their language. b. Germanic, Teutonic. 2. Of or pertaining to the Middle Ages, medieval. Skip points 3a, b and c, waffling on about architecture and settle for . . . 4. Sometimes small g, Of, or pertaining to or reminiscent of a literary style prevalent in the late 18th and early 19th centuries which emphasised the grotesque, mysterious and desolate.

Perfect, particularly the last word. And now, without further Sade Adu, let us set aside our Holy Etruscan Snoods and concentrate on the reigning bands that sulk under the critical clouds.

THE CULT
HAIR TODAY, GONE TOMORROW?

Right: "Fat Man", S.D.C's only vinyl, boosted their reputation. (The hats got better also.)

Below: Southern Death Cult. Pre-metal days, Ian Astbury (foreground) was a renegade sound brave. It didn't last long.

And, as the strains of metal fatigue . . . *fade away*, we recall our old pal Sir Walter Scott who said, not to me personally, 'O what a tangled web we weave, when first we practise to deceive', for what are The Cult if not masters of *self*-deception? The Mister Men of Rock, during six strenuously unpredictable years they have made music that has at times been quite magnificent but rendered insignificant by their latter-day insistence of scrambling towards Rock's apex and chasing the dinosaur's tail, pausing for a fresh identity crisis every time Ian Astbury tries on a new hat.

Their status in this book has been devalued both by rumours of a split and by their stolid march into the quicksands of creative atrophy that rock demands; a melodic slaughterhouse and a tragic *waste* of their talents. While they never achieved anything truly *staggering* during their earlier, fizzier years, they were at least convincing. Most of us hadn't even seen *Spinal Tap*. Now they come over as a flamboyantly correct *outfit* in search of a good video.

Astbury is the historical link through all Cultish periods. He it was that looked and spoke the strangest in the early roar of Southern Death Cult, formed during 1982 and jumping swiftly on to Situation 2 Records for the one solitary single, 'Fat Man', and onto the tip of everyone's tongues, which went nowhere near their cheeks. Pink round the gills he spoke with pride, of sentiments picked up through fascination with Red Indian culture, intrinsic in his quest for individualism. Several years later he wore

the Iron Cross, a badge given to Hitler's finest destroyers of innocent mankind, a symbol later liberated by the equally charmless Hell's Angels. Naïve, romantic, internally confused, Ian Astbury is very strange.

In one sense it should be only the early years that concern us in this book but little would be proved by tackling what they now themselves disown, and their overall descent into hairy turpitude makes for a far more enthralling spectacle of the absurd. What they *have* done simply isn't enough. What they *haven't* done, considering the possibilities, is appalling. These are not the words of some embittered clown who thinks they should be re-peddling their initial wares, this is someone who thinks their fuselage is badly twisted. If they want to rock at least let them do it with hair-singeing *ferocity*, not bumbling about like a bubble car on heat.

In May 1982 Ian Astbury said to *ZigZag's* Tony D, ''. . . it's not just a show. I personally try to put a bait there to draw people, they get the grasp and hopefully start thinking why? . . . to find out about themselves and for the rest of their lives really be into it.'' These days he says something along the lines of ''Yewwww AAAwwwwwrrriiittteeee?'', and makes considerably more sense.

He took Southern Death Cult as far as he thought they could go, the equivalent of a two stop bus journey, before moving on to form Death Cult, involving his main sidekick Billy Duffy, once guitar virtuoso with Theatre Of Hate, and Ray Mondo (drums) and Jamie Stewart (bass) from Ritual. Ray didn't last long, and joined Sex Gang, being replaced by the erratic Nigel Preston. Fleshing out the visceral sounds of S.D.C. with some stodgier infusions,

Above: Bandanarama! A band in search of a Freeman's catalogue!

Left: Never mind the 'Southern', here's Death Cult. Ian, minus hat, with (clockwise) Jamie Stewart, Raymondo and Billy Duffy.

Over page: The Cult. Nigel Preston (second from right) joins the ranks. Ian perfects his Cochisecake image.

17

they released 'The Brothers Grimm' EP and a single, 'God's Zoo', got well into Vietnam imagery and wobbled along quite well, before calling themselves simply The Cult.

With 'Spiritwalker', their début album, the pot-noddling 'Dreamtime', and the sinuous bluster of 'Go West' they took off, their audience swelling appreciably, headlining hither and thither, beaming straight into the sun, when an intangible whirlwind turned Ian Astbury's head around. Imperceptible though it seemed at the time, he was becoming a hippy! Offset only by Billy's calming, brilliantly deadpan, influence, he was ripe for slagging, and deservedly so.

Shortly before they started slipping sneakily off the rails I obtained some assertive snippets from them, not least Billy's ''We're the best band in the world'', followed by Ian's more *gentle* thoughts.

''We want to play to everybody, 14-year-old girls and 35-year-old couples. When I was in Southern Death Cult my head wasn't really in the independent scene, I was just in a group doing my thing and that was that. All of a sudden people said, 'Positive Punk, Independent. Smack! Crap! You Can't Go Out Of These Four Walls!' And I started to believe it. So when I started to try and break away from it I was waiting for someone to go, 'You're an arsehole!'. Then after a while I thought, 'Fuck this, we don't need it!'

''We've just worked hard, made our mistakes and corrected them. It's hard because six months ago no-one knew what we were doing. I think people shied away from us because they thought we were on a megalomania trip.''

'Trip'? People stared, aghast, at the sight of Ian on 'Whistle Test', blowing a whistle, *and* his wavering reputation,

during a gruelling version of 'Resurrection Joe', which was nothing compared to the video for 'She Sells Sanctuary', combining the look of the Robert Louis Stevenson period with an advert involving dogs and loo paper; not so much a bandana as the Invisible Man disintegrating, something The Cult would prove singularly adept at doing. That visual tumour took away from the vitality of the song, a shame, as their 'Love' album generally was a completely flaccid receptacle. Billy Duffy, immediately the album was out and discussed, pointed out how the sound of 'Dreamtime' now made him vomit, a hysterical reaction, mainly because of an overt speediness about it that only he could detect. 'Love' was one of the Hippyest albums most people had ever heard. Disgust was in the air, and the sallow *steel* of 'Rain', another single, also suffered by association. Les Warner, their new drummer, had no such problems with credibility. He had once played for Julian Lennon. Rock and Roll!

Stadia-bound, the subtlety hosed away from the nucleus, the powdery proclamations and lyrical ingenuity drenched by humdrum insousiance, their big noses hardened, attracted by the sweet smell of success in all its glory, moolah and, as would be the creative downfall of The Mission, a taste for Led Zeppelin. As Ian told NME's Richard Cook, he had only stumbled across this band in 1986. "It was a brand new sound to me," he said. "There's nothing else to listen to!"

On one of those rip-off interview albums, more expansive comments are made.

"I feel I'm rebelling against the bad things that are going on," Ian says, "same as everyone else, but I think it's foolish to lead revolutions. All these *supposed* revolutions in music and nothing's changed!"

Nor are they likely to when you walk in reverse. (Maybe if I used a quill?)

"I think our songs are just the best,"

Above left: No grizzly bear on earth could beat him!

Above right: A rare shot of Billy Duffy having nothing to say. (Seldom has there been such a quotable guitarist.)

Right: The Cult on 'The Tube' (R.I.P. thankfully.) A ripsnorter!

20

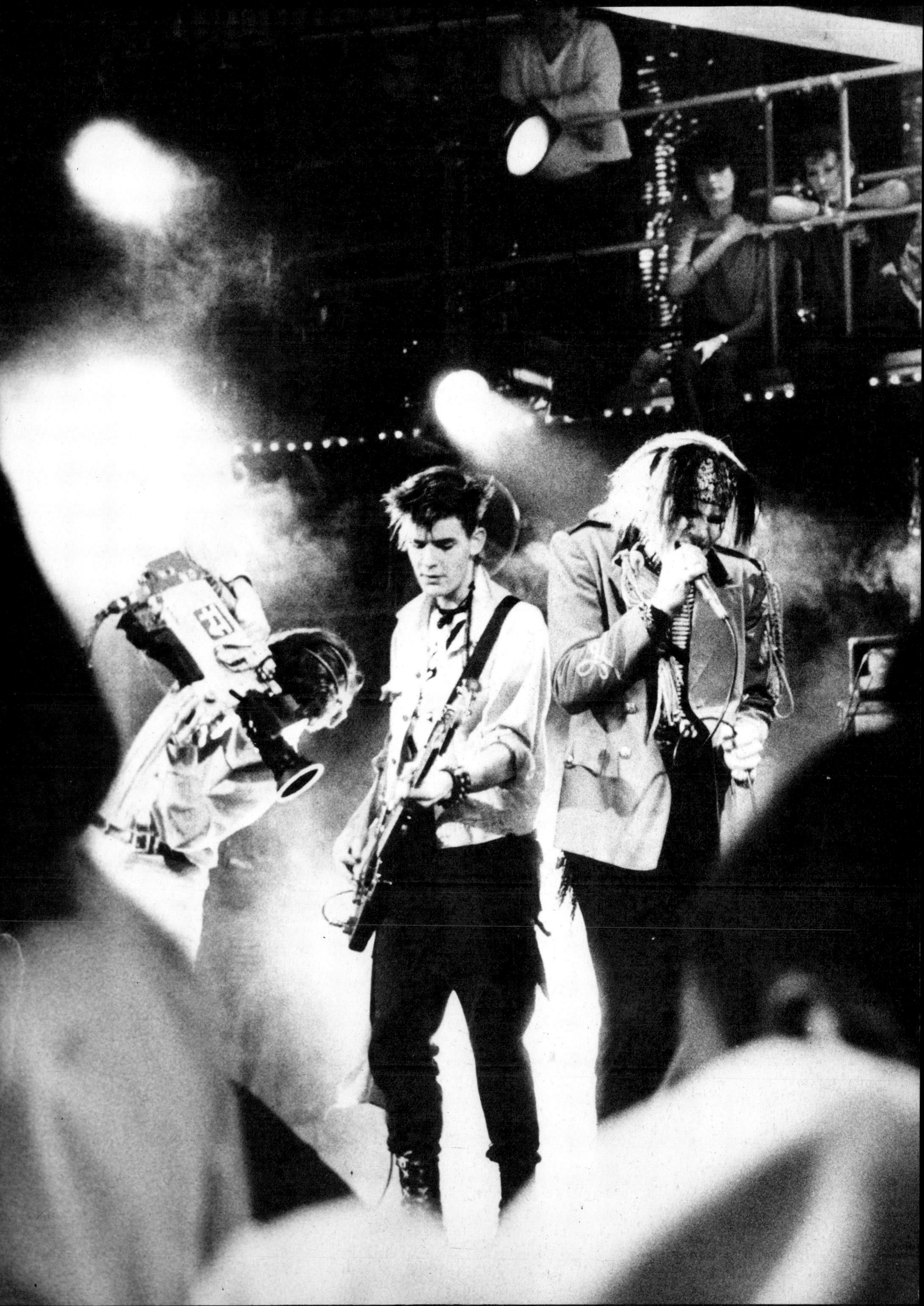

Billy adds, always the shy boy of the two. "The *business*! We do things that nobody else would ever dream of doing 'cos they haven't got the strength inside themselves, like getting a wah-wah pedal out of the closet and going, 'This sounds mental, sounds insane!' and people are going 'Wah-wah pedal? Jimi Hendrix! They're Hippies!' It's like, wait a minute, hold on, we're just using what's available, taking basic sounds to enhance our songs."

Wait a minute. Hold on!!! Maybe Billy's got something there. (Pause.) Nope, he's talking utter drivel, but it was close. By opting for outright conformity, *with* the past, The Cult opened up gaps in their songwriting which should have been sealed. There is usually a water-tight strength to their compositions, but following 'Love' with the gutsier metal drive of 'Electric' they exchanged one set of mindbending rules for another. Moving the way they do, if they're not careful, they could be seeing the 1990s in as leaders of a new Merseysound revival! It's delineation of dignity we're talking about here, and The Cult haven't a clue. By serving a Rock apprenticeship in public at all times, instead of privately, their mistakes scream after them, for they are bigger than most young bands and therefore any errors of judgement will immediately *appear* gigantic, as has been the case.

It isn't fair but it *is* unavoidable. They are the pilot equivalent of someone ditching a Cessna, selecting a Jumbo, then landing at entirely the wrong airport. If they stay together, a big *if* the way things are going, they'll make some cracking singles two years hence, but not until their own identity lumbers out of this self-imposed fog of disarray.

Right: "Not now Ian, not now. We'll save the levitation for later."

Below: Astbury survives the rubber glove test.

When they recorded 'Electric' their first version was by all accounts, particularly their own, absolute tripe. Admitting all to Carol Clerk of *Melody Maker*, they laughed, ''We couldn't decide what to do. The penny was beginning to drop that you can't polish a turd. Something was fundamentally wrong with the way we'd recorded the songs.''

Multi-talented and exceedingly hip Rick Rubins came sprinting to the rescue blabbing on about more *potent* rock sensibilities, a man noted for his hard edge. It still remains a flawed album, as anything given the kiss of life would, but at least it crackled with its fair share of big, bad *beauty* and it gave us 'Lil' Darlin' which was agreeable enough, in a 'Prime Mover' way, except that it had a straight face.

Of the sound, Ian smooched towards

Main pic: Unbeknown to Les Warner and Jamie Stewart, Ian and Billy have become one!

Left top: In keeping with their enormous appeal overseas, particularly the Americas, Billy's hair became quite unmanageable.

Left centre and bottom: "Hello. Bilbo Baggins is the name."

Neil Perry of *Sounds*, suggesting, "It's definitely more sensual. We stripped away all the contraceptives and got to the grunt and grind of it. In the past we haven't felt so good about ourselves because we haven't been totally convinced by what we've put on record."

Oh, really! I think we've heard that excuse before. What'll it be next time? Let's hope this honesty stays consistent after 'Electric'. Let's also hope that Jamie stops getting shunted about like some ticklish errand boy, having been booted on to extra guitar at one point when Zodiac's Kid Chaos joined as bassist, only to leave with a grim taste in his mouth, followed later by a furious Les Warner. In The Cult camp Ian and Billy have been pissing on the fire! "On the way to one of the last video shoots," Les confided to *Sounds*' Mary Anne Hobbs, "Billy told me

Above: "Revolution Joe" period. Billy and Ian, sharp enough to cut any rug.

Right: One of these men is wearing embarrassing footwear. (It's up to you, readers!)

he'd like to get Ian out of the band. So who knows, maybe Billy has plans to become a solo artist.''

Unlikely I would have thought. The Cult have now got to concentrate on producing memorable music. Doing something right for once. One monumentally strong record will wipe clean the slate because everyone is bored with their past pollutants. They have it in them, if they have the inclination. Far from being the fiercely pedantic band we have come to expect, with a sweet line in smoothing over their awesome blunders, they are sensible people at heart, possibly just over-awed at the size their operation

has become and the inherent complexities of the task itself, such as thinking for yourself.

When they wise up and stop looking up at the stars, they'll do the best thing possible, what can be termed position 31, a 'Billy Idol', making truly sonic pop music. They can't handle the Rock side, they failed the Goth test, as they wanted to, but having left so many different looks and personnel scattered behind them on the trail they are beginning to seem like a grief-stricken caravan lost in the desert.

Why are their arms always down the toilet? Because they don't know their arse from their elbow.

THE SISTERS OF MERCY
BORN TO BE RILED

Of *all* those propelled towards infamy for their purveyance of primarily dark imagery there is no-one to match the intangible presence of the thin white fluke, Andrew Eldritch, the voice behind the shades that are ominously synonymous with The Sisters Of Mercy. Through seven years of fluctuating activity, with a little help from his hairpin bends, he has leapt clear, in agonising slow motion, of indie intransigence, illness, ill feeling and inertia into the often sycophantic arms of the press and the ears of a nation. Abrim with deceits, clinging somewhat impishly to the image of a fearful bounder, for all the silvered lances thrust into his highly unlikely rib-cage he has proved impossible to pin down. An intriguing mind and therefore an interesting creator, he casts a brooding menace over listless chart territory and nothing, short of a sniper's bullet, can stop him now, as *befits* the only known descendant of the Ancient Mariner.

His trickling tale truly begins in Leeds, the city which would prove to be a spawning ground for an enormous, yawning, Goth production line. Indeed, it is said, quietly, that if you laid all the Goths in Leeds end to end the police steamroller would have a field day. The Sisters Of Mercy, formed in 1981, were ahead of the pack and remain that way.

Eldritch's introduction to music did not follow a traditional course, as he explains on a recent, unofficial, 'interview' album. "I never had any musical talent at all," he states. "I was banned from music classes and told I would never, ever, be able to understand anything and I was quite prepared to accept that. I *couldn't* play the recorder! I still don't think I can sing but somehow I get away with it."

With a brain the size of a bottle-bank, Eldritch did develop a keen interest in languages, which enabled him to become a dreaming spire himself, at Oxford.

"Then Leeds. There's only six places in Great Britain where you can learn Chinese at university and Leeds was one of them."

Nailing himself to Mandarin Chinese, necessitating practical work in Peking, his enthusiasm dimmed, as a year of virtual incarceration held few thrills.

"They don't let you see very much. You *can* go off and see a tractor farm! It gets to 30 degrees below in winter. Didn't *really* fancy it."

At the age of 21 somebody thoughtfully stored their drum kit in the cellar of Eldritch's home. Uneven noises, pummelled with gusto, soon rent the rarefied atmosphere and a reputation was gained as the one man in Leeds who refused to dally with cymbals or torture

Andrew Eldritch in the Andrex advert that went badly wrong.

the tom-toms. He was asked to provide the rhythmical axis for what would become the first Sisters record.

"I just wanted to sound like the Glitter Band," he claims. "Nothing else. I was really very happy doing that, but then the guy that asked me to play drums decided he wasn't very good at singing and he insisted that I have a go and because we couldn't buy a machine that could do the singing but we *could* buy a machine to do the drums . . . that's what happened."

With Gary Marx and Benn Gunn on guitar, Eldritch on overdrive, Craig 'Lerch' Adams on bass and the drum machine, christened Doktor Avalanche, the first single, 'Damage Done', slipped out on the vaguely hip CNT label.

Pastily pop, remarkably, this had little to recommend it other than some sweetly curving guitar and a desire to melt, so it wasn't until the follow up, 'Body Electric'/ 'Adrenochrome' that dandruff and déjà-vu were banished beneath the taut notoriety of gushing energy. Eldritch, already the band's spokesman, a bicycle wheel spoke for a generation, bent the ear of *Melody Maker's* Adam Sweeting shortly before the single's release.

"There was one great heavy metal group and that was The Stooges, and there's only two bands around that can touch them, and they're Motorhead and The Birthday Party. We're not as good as Motorhead but we're better than The Birthday Party. That makes us pretty damn good."

Ambitions, it seems, were held pretty damn low!

Although sporty in their approach The Sisters had emerged decidedly spotty in appearance. Clearly what they needed was building up, as any band worth its salt tax was similarly adept at channelling

their molecules into precise parcels of paranoia. 'Alice', the third single, released on their own Merciful Release label without CNT assistance, was an altogether more civilised affair; the hectic power kept to a steady tick, the melody — an important discovery — far stronger, so much larger than before.

Eldritch, aghast that people should ever compare him to the translucent King of the Goths, Peter Murphy of Bauhaus, cannot deny that an accidental likeness exists here. Less gruff, more entwined in an archly dramatic vocal style, he almost *is* Bela's number one fan. (At the time Eldritch was also compared frequently to the corpses of Jim Morrison and The Psychedelic Furs' Richard Butler.) How we laughed, while also impressed by the volcanic tar pit on the flip, entitled 'Floorshow'. Once again it was Adam Sweeting, the first to take them seriously, who slapped his Walkman on to the table. An eclectic can of worms was promptly opened.

"Well basically it involves the dialectics of cynicism," Eldritch said, confirming *exactly* what we all thought lay at the pert bottom of their allegedly humorous elements. Openly contemptuous of their 'Goth' peers, blessed with a roguishly pale name (half nun, half prostitute: highly original! *Snort!*), with cover artwork designed by Eldritch himself and apparently ripped off, the band even claimed that their freewheeling destructive moments on stage bordered on 'slapstick'. If it wasn't for an evident intelligence more restless than their two-dimensional contemporaries, you could only conclude that the band were *detergents provocateurs*.

". . . to us cynicism is very closely linked to faith," Eldritch continued, "or

Fields Of The . . . whoops, it's Andrew Eldritch again, laughing while Rome burns.

31

The Sisters, displaying the sartorial elegance that would play no part in their ever increasing success.

belief, or holding anything dear. It's the sort of cynicism that comes out of disappointment with one's environment rather than a despair of it, and that's a very precious thing — it isn't something to lose. It's the only thing which separates us from bozos.''

Segregated by purely academic arrogance, they toiled away with their rickety racket, supporting those bands they usually found alarmingly banal, such as UK Decay, Sex Gang Children, Gun Club (remember that name) and even Aswad! Hushed, garbled, blushing reviews resulted, accepting that the Sisters at least had something different steaming from their armpits, accessibility made easier by the release of 'Anaconda', a peek at heroin's increasing presence, which was nothing new, given their penchant for polite panoramas of pustular grace, but once again the B-side, 'Phantom', had a crumpled ace up its sleeve, when Doktor Avalanche twinned himself with Ian Astbury's fevered imagination and turned Red Indian for an afternoon.

1983 turned out to be quite a year for The Sisters. Hot on the scabby heels of 'Anaconda' came the catatonic coupling of the 'Reptile House' EP and another squirming seven incher, 'Temple Of Love'. 'Gonzoid Amphetamine Filth Is Dead' ran the cryptic run-out groove message and so it was! These were queasily quiet records. They were destined for the top of the indie charts with indecent haste.

These songs spluttered and twisted, intoxicated by their own toxins, a churning, restless energy waiting below decks. 'Temple Of Love' struck a particularly sinuous pose, flexing muscles previously left wasted, opening up like a vulture's mouth to reveal a

purple worm dancing on a charred polyester tongue. The band were now headlining in their own right (supported by The Smiths in their coyly flirtatious apprenticeship and the blustery Flesh For Lulu), with large record companies attracted by the nefarious pop menu.

Benn Gunn, in a move which failed to trouble seismologists anywhere, then decided he had had enough and left the band, either unimpressed or unaware of the cunning deal The Sisters were negotiating with WEA, whereby the power of artistic decisions lay firmly in the band's sweaty fist. Jayne Houghton, a *ZigZag* photographer/reporter, eventually tracked Gunn down to a trendy Leeds public house.

''The general band policies, which are obviously derived from one member, began to stink,'' he insisted. ''I'm going to Liverpool to do a degree because the whole music business stinks.''

Benn, obviously a man with a sensitive nose, did start a label, Flame On Records, as well as the illusory band Torch, which failed to light. Gunn also failed to rise to Jayne's diplomatic suggestion that he was an obnoxious git.

''Maybe, Jayne, maybe,'' he sweet-talked. ''I had it in me to get out of The Sisters. They were always taking the piss out of the system, which was why I was *in* the band, until they started taking themselves seriously. Now they're no better than anyone else. Worse, in fact. They're just not funny any more. So I got out . . . but I'll be back.''

As we ponder the question, Where is Benn Gunn *now*, we also acknowledge that his replacement turned out to be a precociously hairy young thing called Wayne Hussey, late of the tempestuously adequate Dead Or Alive (itself an

Early days, yet even then their hair was terrifying.

extension of Pete Burns's original Goth extravaganza, Nightmares In Wax).

Despite Hussey's early resemblance to a stunted John Cooper-Clarke, this was a timely union, providing more contoured monochrome to the existing wheezing hump of hilarity, his own songwriting flair producing added zest which was just the dog-eared ticket considering the higher stakes and heavier grillings which accompanied their first WEA-linked singles, 'Body And Soul' and 'Walk Away' — pallid and plump respectively — which inched their way up the charts. Not far enough, *but* far enough, if you see what I mean. (Nobody becomes Rick Astley overnight.)

Mr Spencer, everyone's favourite loveable spiky-top at *Sounds*, could barely control his waterworks when documenting this vigorous period under the amused stare of the Eldritch spectre. He ventured the torrid suggestion that Eldritch was one of the world's biggest bastards. Equally jovial, Eldritch replied, "I mean, I don't even go to the corner shop without figuring, 'Hey! Here goes Andrew Eldritch to the corner shop. This is, you know, some kind of big deal to someone' . . ."

Britain's most articulate stick insect was relaxed during this interview, as you would expect from a man who would perform '1969' (Stooges) and Hot Chocolate's 'Emma' on any one given night.

"My world is divided into Us, Them and people I don't talk to," he told Mr 'Us' Spencer. (I come under categories two *and* three!) "Most of the world is actually 'us', and I do try and be nice to us, although I think the only way you can get to give something useful to the 'us's of this world is by being a bastard to the 'them's, because really they are there to be bastards to you, and this is not a world for the weak-willed."

So perhaps Mr Spencer, grin extending, was right to be surprised by the admission that old Hatty Japes himself got nervous before hitting the stage, his bowels every bit as jittery as the next shadow.

"Always, because I never figured I was cut out for this sort of work and I always have to sort of figure out . . . God! How am I doing? Not as well as I'd like, because one never is.

"The whole Sisters Of Mercy jigsaw," Mr Spencer heard, "is kind of tough. I know what it is in my head, but I've never really been able to articulate it in any one way. It's like I've got a solitary coherent idea at the back of my head. I find various diffuse ways of expressing it . . ."

The buggers charted with their long-awaited début album, delayed due to Eldritch's attack of fatigue which not only laid him lower than normal but also brought some drastic re-examination of his seriously debilitating approach to life. (Called suicidal tendencies.) Only the ultra-churlish would complain about the success granted to such songs as the title track, 'First Last And Always', the sweetness of 'Black Planet' or the blight of 'A Rock And A Hard Place', although the attendant single 'No Time To Cry' seemed decidedly iffey.

In another memorable exchange, this time with *Melody Maker's* Steve Sutherland, Eldritch avoided the topic of the album but several interesting facts emerged, from the possession of a copy of 'Careless Whisper', support for the woeful Manchester United, Jimmy White and even Jake Thackeray, once semi-immortal for his song 'Sister Josephine'!

Spooky just *isn't* the word. Ironic may be the best word for *this* snippet passed Steve's way.

"We're in a good position to achieve what we want with regard to the mainstream. We can step in and out of it as required and the band decide what's required, not someone else."

The Sisters plunged onwards, a band decision growing ever closer, busting their landing gear over a British tour, visiting the States and returning for more gigs, including their best remembered, at the Royal Albert Hall. Pomp's head fell to the sneaky blade of circumstance when

the band split up. Nobody knew what the hell was going on.

Later, in another head-to-head with Steve Sutherland, Eldritch pinpointed the main trouble spot as the American tour. Returning from a week-long break in Mexico, he became blessed by the thought, "God, what are those people whingeing about, really? They just got so feeble. Then they said, 'Well, okay, what are we gonna do for new songs?' and I said 'How about this, this and this' and unfortunately the first 'this' I cited had too many chords per minute and Craig said, 'If that's the guitar line I'm not

Mean, broody . . . magnificent!

playing it' and walked out.''

Entertaining Neil Perry over at *Sounds* the brazen Hussey told the story in a slightly different fashion.

''We got to doing the second album and Andrew said 'I'm not singing any of your songs'. That's what it boils down to. Craig walked out of rehearsals and a day later I did. He was listening to things like Fleetwood Mac, Stevie Nicks, Foreigner and there was us listening to Motorhead or whatever. And it showed.''

Who was it said, 'It's the sort of cynicism that comes out of disappointment with one's environment rather than a despair of it'?

Anyway, Hussey seems unflustered. Insisting to Perry that The Sisters were nothing *but* a joke, made bearable by their appreciation of history, he also added, ''the thing about Eldritch . . . is, he's dried up.''

The desiccated singer thought otherwise. Having moseyed around his much loved Germany and America his plans turned once again towards music, particularly when he discovered that Hussey and Adams, together with former Artery man Simon Hinkley and Red Lorry Yellow Lorry's Mick Brown had gathered

''I stopped them using the name The Sisters. Then my lawyer told me that if they *wanted* to be called The Sisterhood there was nothing I could do about it, so I

wearing a suit and telling tales of working with Jim Steinman (Meatloaf's Godsend), *and* a choir, we didn't so much raise eyebrows as the proverbial roof, with gales of uproarious laughter.

That turned out to be called 'This Corrosion'. Now where *did* I put that calorie-reduced hat?

Crashing into the Top 10 without so much as a by-your-leave and accompanied by an unbelievably garish video – except for one 'rain'-soaked moment when Eldritch truly *was* Michael Jackson – this was a petulant swordfish comeback as a hammerhead shark, revelling in dizzying petrol fumes. The New York Choral Society sail in and out like a portacommunion as Morrison's bass, a shadowy tea clipper of a rhythmical tool, quite the warmest instrument ever to grace a Sisters record, highlighted only too clearly why this version of The Sisters beats the crap out of the predecessor. You no longer feel encased in gauze, and the components are breathing freely. It can make you feel by turns skittish and irresponsible or a hundred bloody years old; something *worth* listening to rather than merely dissecting.

With 'Dominion' the Morrison contribution blossoms further, if that *is* her vocal support we hear counterbalancing Eldritch's own Lee Marvin anecdotal evidence. His grazed opulence provides many a remarkable moment, particularly the wonderfully, improbably, ventilated 'Lucretia' single; his husky tones like mustard gas filtered through a wedding dress.

Steve Sutherland asked whether he was still taking the piss.

''Well of course I'm taking the piss – it's the only way to be serious about it. Same

settling for defeat. Then they called themselves The Mission.

Eldritch meanwhile teamed up with one time Gunclubbing bass person Patricia Morrison and as far as we, the great unearthed, were concerned, they had disappeared. Perhaps if I developed my theory that the very name Eldritch is a bastardisation of 'Edrich', as in John, as in son of Bill, a magnificently staunch English batsman, it could do something to alleviate my embarrassment. No? I thought not.

Stage two of The Sisters story could not have been more unorthodox. When the initial, unnerving, news circulated that Eldritch had been spotted near his Ladbroke Grove managerial retreat,

Left: What is it with these people and their hats?!

Far left: Poltergeist IV.

as it ever was.''

Fine. Except, exploitation, with or without his consent, is rife. There are different single mixes, both here and abroad, sufficient to bankrupt any collector, as well as limited edition/ imagination picture disc interview singles *sets* (!) and, most obnoxious of all, a CD interview record housed in an album-sized box. A man who takes the piss can just as easily drown in it.

There is little of the 'bastard' in his actual lyrics of course, they sound ripped, worn and kindly. If he truly does feel like an animal, deep inside, it is only a stuffed salamander. You can take work on such a large scale in one way, staring at the air between your speakers as though a rare stained glass window were about to appear. The haughty, draughty imagery fails to take the listener very far at all. All too personal. You can *only* listen.

So who *is* this creature who currently demands so much attention? Is he, as many vicars believe, Lawrence Of Arabia, reduced to moped status? Is he Flashman, with a bad attack of wind, or is he perhaps A. J. Raffles with a fist-sized wart on the end of his nose? No, he is not. Nor is he remotely close to his own preferred list of Torquemada, Syd Barrett updated and Tony Hancock. He is all things to all farmyard impressionists, as they bay and squawk for his eye, like scatterbrained parrots inside a suitcase, all of them blithely unaware that he comes from a purely literary nest.

It would be interesting, providing Sting was banished discreetly from the set, should anyone even have the courage to tackle Peake's 'Gormenghast' in its true filthy richness, to see Eldritch play the part he was born for. Eldritch, thin as a lie, swordstick in hand, really *is* the scuttling Steerpike. First he drives you to distraction. Then he expects a tip!

THE MISSION
THE GREAT ESCAPE

Fortune certainly favours the unshaved, and who *better* to prove this gorgeously pointed point but those tousled, testifying, death-defying terrapins, The Mission? Gathered together when last we met, under a banner of bravado, their Motorhead and Led Zeppelin albums tucked under one arm, a curious throbbing in their heads under the other, the future must have seemed a tad unpredictable, yet their pursuit had purpose, what with scores to settle, hair to grow and *something to prove.* Success came easily, but the vomit-strewn journey has not been without copious dilemmas, for The Mission *are* a puzzled rock band, with all the ensuing personality pangs through excess and a gluttony for the past.

The biggest shock of all is that they've only been going for three years, when it seems a great deal longer. That's not an insult either and I am hardly the only one confused. "We're not hippies," Wayne Hussey informed a credulous crowd in mid-'87, when cheesecloth and ashes *threatened*, voguishly, to become endemic. "We're *punks.*" Oh get along with you!

They're an odd bunch all round. Mick Brown, previously drummer behind the angry grey confines of Red Lorry Yellow Lorry had already performed benefit gigs with Wayne and Craig, so that trio were comfy-bumfy — positively ecstatic when Simon Hinkley completed the foursome, having left the often hysteria-ridden Artery, but it is Wayne himself with the oldest secret, which has nothing to do with his period as Dead or Alive's unruly sentinel. It is much funnier.

Perhaps the next time you're passing a specialist record shop you might care to slip inside and ask for a copy of 'A Trip To The Dentist', a compilation album released in 1980. There you can stare foolishly at the cover photograph of all the artistes involved and wonder which of the impossibly dorkish contingent might be Wayne. It isn't easy. Then you hear a block of airhead rock/pop wafer entitled 'And The Dance Goes On' and the crime worsens. This, the sleeve notes inform us, was 'Written on a car trip between Porthcawl and Bristol'. Christ, he must have been doing over a hundred miles an hour! Live fast, cry young.

Six years on, Wayne and his chums were finding it easy to pack out the gigs, the reason for those initially troublesome events being confided to *Melody Maker*'s own hairy lunatic, Mat Smith, Mission aficionado. "I knew it would antagonise Andrew," Wayne tittered. "And we also got a lot of press out of it. I always knew we'd lose the battle but we didn't see it as a battle as such — more of a publicity stunt." The rascal! (If Eldritch is even half the man he pretends to be he ought to be highly supportive of such methods.)

"Our songs are a lot more accessible than The Sisters ever were," Wayne continued. "The criteria we use in The Mission is that if it sounds good when we play it on an acoustic guitar in my living room. That's how the song 'Serpent's Kiss' began life. The majority of the songs we've been doing in the set so far are my songs that Andrew rejected for the second Sisters' album. It's ironic 'cos he actually saw us in Birmingham and told us how good he thought the songs were."

Laugh? Er, no . . . not really, because 'Serpent's Kiss', released on knowledgeable indie Chapter 22 Records, is little more than a winsome potboiler, easily overshadowed by the majority of what would become their début album.

Right: Wayne Hussey, wondering what's so difficult about this busking lark.

Over page: The Mission. THE MISH! Clean shaven, if nothing else.

That was May 1986 for you. Bloody typical. The Cult's audience were, according to Wayney Wayney Wayney (copyright: Chris Roberts) ripe for the plucking, which The Mission did, harvesting fit to burst. As the rest of the indie scene was still soiled by the jangling, post-shambling excrement that would finally die as cutie-pop, people seeking *noise* didn't have too many alternatives. Top guitar commandos, almost.

Garnished by a string arrangement from Adam Peters, the July release of 'Garden Of Delight' was a strange choice, being neither massively melodic, preferring to crawl along, nor particularly demanding in pace or atmosphere. It was monstrously pleasant, but isn't everything these days?

The first *big* single was 'Stay With Me', their first for Mercury, via the new Phonogram deal. Swirling petite nuances gild the large-boned hookline that stays in *deep*, with a similarly ravishing B-side 'Blood Brother'. In yet another Mat Smith encounter, Hussey was in joyous mood.

''It annoys me,'' he said, annoyed, ''that people think that just because you've signed to a major you've lost your character.''

(A Major: ''Poppycock dear boy, give it to 'em straight!'')

''It's the critic's artistic licence to give us a hammering,'' he continued, bruises healing easily, ''just as it's ours to release records that annoy them. Also I think that we can get away with it to a certain degree because we've got so much *more* character than most of the bands around today.''

Questioned about potential rockist tendencies, à la Cult, he conjured up a beautiful quote, steaming with

45

Above: I've got a nice hat too!

Right: The only way is UP!

Over page: Wayne Hussey, modelling one of Dana's old cast-offs.

horrendous imagery.

"I'd like to *fuck* Ian Astbury but I don't want to be him."

Quite. Moving swiftly on then . . .

November 1986 saw the release of the collectively mottled but grandly titled 'God's Own Medicine' album, produced by Tim Palmer and recorded in less than two months. ('And The Dance Goes On' is exhumed!) Unfortunately, there is a tendency to cram the background with unnecessary contributions and the excessive vocal stew of 'Bridges Burning' must have seemed like a good idea *once*. 'Let Sleeping Dogs Die' and 'Love Me To Death' crankily disrupt the general flow of piquant energy but the rest is spot on, a stately romp. The flickering spleen of 'Dance On Glass', the wickedly nervous

'Sacrilege' and a wispy 'Severina', featuring the happy warbling of All About Eve's Julianne Regan (one of several forays provided) creep deliriously into the medal positions behind the monster of an opening track which we shall get to later.

Robin Gibson, cantankerous *Sounds* cavalier, explored with Wayne the religious side of things, for Wayne is a baptised Mormon, though not a practising one, claiming that his study of religion has given him his own code of conduct. Verily, we imagine, one must throw up at every available opportunity. Why else would the *Melody Maker* offices need to be sluiced out and fumigated after Wayne and Craig had nipped in to review the singles, redecorating the floor in the process? Ah, but I digress. Back to Robin's probing, if he'll pardon the phrase.

"I think I was very extreme when I was younger," Wayne believed, "in a religious sense. I used to have evenings spent in church when other kids were out playing football and screwing girls . . . the other three in the group — they were *lads*, they've all been done for being drunk and disorderly when they were 16. That to me is normal. I can see my life as a youngster was extreme. But then again, most 27-year-olds don't do what I do either, aren't as extreme as I am now . . ."

Perhaps that's just as well . . .

Extreme or not this Hussey is also a charming chap who buried his hamster, Ashville, when it was obviously dead, with all its little toys. I think that's far sadder and lovelier than The Mission's current predicament, which *at the time* would have been unthinkable, as January 1987 saw the release of one of the Eighties' truly *great* singles, 'Wasteland'. Choc full of piffling verbal smokescreens

it features the unforgettable, 'Heaven
And Hell', I know them well, but I haven't
yet made my choice. I'm feeling scared,
'cos I'm shouting loud and *no-one* can
hear my voice'. The strolling bass is
welded to cautious drums and the
niggling guitar niceties tinge rather than
drench the song (often a problem of
theirs). It is harder than a Bolivian toasted
sandwich and brighter than
Michaelangelo's nose, deserving a higher
station than the paltry number 11 it
reached in the charts. Sobbing to *RM's*
Vici MacDonald, Wayne admitted, ''When
we didn't get on to *Top Of The Pops* and
the record went down from 11 to 13
I curled up over there (tour bus priest's
hole) and cried for four hours. I really
did.'' The wimp!

'Severina' got them there easily
enough, proudly gormless in their
posture, with Julianne Regan giving a fine
display inside her designer bogey. Things
at this point were fine, other than the bad
reputation their most central following —
The Eskimos — were beginning to attract,
mainly one of gratuitous violence and
blatant stupidity. The chicken dancer's
lament? There can often be this danger
with bands who first foster clandestine
support, that their hardcore following
will resent and reject 'outsiders', to the

extent of becoming obstreperous, even violent, and such was the torrent of complaints that once again Mat Smith was called upon to strap on his laser-operated codpiece, with X-Raying attachment, and get sleuthing. Originally, it transpires, they were simply known as The Missionaries, a quaint enough position. Then they became the Sausage Squad. Well, what else? Finally, thanks to a deranged European border guard, The Eskimos. Mat found only a gregarious ebullience in the crowd, although the Mish themselves spoke of the dangers of warped loyalty. (Nutters in other words.)

Wayne: "When we were in Berlin last time, this weirdo girl came up to me and said, 'Listen, Brian Jones was murdered, Marc Bolan was murdered and you're next on the list'. I said, 'Oh, thank you very much for that piece of information!' She was a real weirdo. She followed us for the whole German tour. It was really frightening.

"I made the mistake of talking to her on the first night 'cos she said, 'Do you like Marc Bolan?' and I said, 'Yeah', she said, 'Good, 'cos I've got something to tell you about him'. I thought 'Good — at least I'll get my end away then'.

"It used to affect me a lot more in the beginning. I'm stronger now. I know I'm a pop personality and I'm prepared to play up to it but, at the same time, I'm not gonna let someone kill me for the sake of some good press."

Which was what one comely American wench had on her mind, informing the band via our genial postal system that Wayne's name spelt backwards amounted somehow to the name of Gary Gilmour and that Hussey could benefit from watching over his shoulder. Strangest of all was the lad who mistook

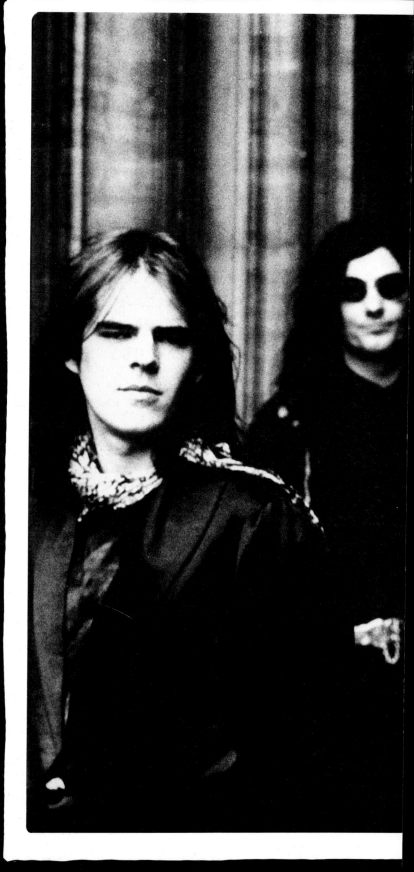

Wayne's spoken intro to the album and promptly sold his soul to the devil — you know, the way you do — and asked him, now that he'd seen the error of his ways, what he should do next! The Mission's life isn't all wine and roses. Sometimes you just can't *find* any roses. Cracks would soon appear, none of them wise.

The band toured America for two-and-a-half months non-stop and their excessive tendencies took over, Wayne admitting later that at least £8,000 was blown on drugs, as well as the boys drinking themselves under any table within a five-mile radius of the band, generally living the life of Old Mother Riley. In Los Angeles one day things got too much for Craig Adams. They had performed a dastardly lunchtime gig at the LA Palace and on returning to the hotel, where he couldn't remember his room number, he threw his boots at the receptionist, insulted the management and for this rapturous performance was clapped in handcuffs by eager policemen. At this point one of the entourage pointed out they might need him for the evening's gig. Wayne takes up the story, as told to MM's Carol Clerk.

"He freaked out then and said, 'I wanna go home. I don't want to be in a band'. At that stage we couldn't do anything for him, and after that I started thinking he was being bloody minded. We said, 'Go home and we'll carry on without you'. I think he expected us to say, 'Let's all go home'. If we'd all *gone* home I don't think we'd be together now."

The tour was completed, with soundman Pete Turner filling the void and when Craig came to his senses everything was sorted out although the American legacy, in the shape of their new album, would still cause problems.

Main pic: Samantha Fox, watch out!

Top left: For self-proclaimed poseurs they're not terribly good at it.

Bottom left: The Boy George comparisons faded out swiftly.

Holy Gurly Sandals,
Batman! This is no
way for a grown man
to dress!

It is hardly unknown for bands who achieve minor stardom to go slightly askew from their original path when they start meeting their heroes and Wayne, who couldn't resist kissing Iggy or cuddling Bono, when the chances presented themselves, is just the kind of character who will let discretion evaporate in the face of his idols. When the band found their own Pope John Paul, the circumspect Mr. Jones, legendary Led Zeppelin bassist, who offered to produce the band, they were in seventh heaven. For all I know they still are. Hussey stopped looking like Boy George coming through a hedge backwards and took on a Bono-ish persona and the album, in the finest Rock Cliché manner, would concern itself with three themes – as opposed to concepts, yah? – children, heat and America. Now I'm not suggesting that fatherhood, which Wayne experienced when his daughter Hannah appeared upon whom he naturally dotes, turned him into a tiresome warhorse, but there is everything about their creative inertia right now which reeks heavily of long term rock sluggishness. When the album, 'Children' did appear, the differences between this and its predecessor couldn't have been more glaring.

The songs were solid, soiled almost in a sanctimonious way, with worrying lethargic innards. From the protracted intro of children's distant voices (Zzzzz), there is a fabricated feel. A gelatinous 'Beyond The Pale' and a totally wasted 'A Wing And A Prayer' needed the friction of desperation *inside* them, not the unenticing brand of a CD *about* them. Early seventies rock lessons return to irritate the listener and both Jones and the band must shoulder the blame.

If you have followed the band through thick and thin then naturally these songs might succeed in bringing back memories but being the supercharged pedestrian plodders that they undoubtedly are, it makes you feel tired as you listen. 'Tower Of Strength', the first single to be taken from the album, simply *pottered* along. Here we have to ponder the role of Jones in all this abundance of finery and total dilution of outright energy. His production is *immaculate*, overturning any exuberance in favour of succulence and suddenly The Mission become old before their time.

"We don't want to sound like Led Zeppelin," Wayne Hussey told a relieved Steve Sutherland, "though I honestly don't know where we stand in the overall scheme of things . . . it's still funny to me that we're pop stars. I mean, we're just a bunch of buffoons."

Heaven and Hell, I know them well and choice doesn't come into it. The Mission, the prime purveyors of what people can justifiably call 'Gothic Rock', in its least pretentious but overstuffed form, should be made to stand in the corner, heads hung low. For all their new-found, somewhat grotesque, beauty on tracks like 'Black Mountain Mist' and 'Hymn (For America)' their records are signifying precisely nothing.

They are like fallen women of the Victorian era, led astray by the elders and 'betters', temporarily deprived of the captaincy of their own destiny. Turn again lads, I say, give up this wanton abdication of responsibility as you merge in with Rock's faded tapestry. Step this way, shedding a few cataracts of distressing compression, into this wind tunnel.

Blow these cobwebs away.

GOTH HISTORY: PART TWO
GOTH BROS

They may well squirm and sulk but four chapters on we are finally reunited with those rascals, Bauhaus. They stepped out of the shadows, agitated and agitating, to cut a livid swathe through the doldrums of the early eighties as a challenging thrill from The Underworld. They *cultivated* vivacity as easily as they invented the wild, exotic mystery that the music required. Nerves of steel. Chart elevation subsequently led to more prurient plateaus but that needn't concern us as I want you to ask yourself the following question: How *many* of what we may reasonably refer to as 'Goth' bands have used onstage what we can only describe as wholly manufactured images, which are essential to their art? Now there's a stiff one. (Typing often has this effect on me!) About one hundred per cent, you say? I won't quibble, because you are obviously right. The imagery, totally dramatic, has to be there. Cloth caps don't cut it! It is a façade, true, but a glorious one. Why else do the audiences constantly find it necessary to plunge or wriggle into skintight nothings, or to encase themselves in voluminous cascades of cloth? This cross-mixing of neo-romanticism and punk/ninja night attire, along with the generally less refined rippling t-shirt brigades is all perfectly and quite horribly tribal. They all want to belong to this silent, until inebriated, *community*, which, as far as I can see, is all quite proper, if only so that you can discern like-minded folk at other palaces of entertainment. The only *real* problem usually occurs inside the Vatican, around Summer, where disbelieving Nephilim fans have to have it explained time and time again that the Shroud Of Turin is *un*connected with the official 'Dawnrazor' merchandising.

It goes backwards and forwards much further than that as well. Look at Marc Almond. Look at Toyah! Rather seedy, isn't it?

It is the simplification of a popular theme. Bauhaus themselves took some of The Banshees' gleam, minus the shattered bearskin of a hairstyle, as the svelte asthmatic Peter Murphy smoothed his hair and had his lean figure defined by brilliantly harsh white light, his image perfected. Earlier, when I saw him in action, supporting the lost Goth giants *Gloria Mundi* (staffed mainly by occasional cabaret 'artistes' Eddie And Sunshine), he looked like a Bowiesque dosser. 'Dark Entries', 'Stigmata Martyr', 'In The Flat Field'. . . how can we ignore them? Latent camp camaraderie, sculptured cheeks and writhing torsos! Legend has it that he needs a keep-net for his testicles. However, resistance was on the upturn and Theatre Of Hate formed, under the auspices of Kirk Brandon's pyramid shaped brain. They picked up the disaffected Killing Joke audience, only to eventually lose it to Death Cult, and so it goes on, crowds moving part and parcel to the new kings of the herd. New Model Army, The Mission and currently The Nephilim. Loyalty doesn't last, it lingers.

Frequently more exciting and free of contaminated poses were Luton's UK Decay, a band that were to become unconscious patrons of this art form, always helping to promote other bands, at their expense of their own nobility. Led by the most engaging of frontmen, Abbo, from their 'Black Cat' EP onwards it was a jagged ride accompanied by a restless smile. 'For Madmen Only', the album, and 'Unexpected Guest' titillated the tastebuds. 'Rising From The Dread', a compulsively twisting 12-inch, ripped

*Slade The Leveller. 'Only Stupid B*****ds wear waistcoats'.*

anyone before them, droning, drowning and charming us all with their sulphurous tones. 4AD caught them in glorious form on the 'Fetisch' album. On Phonogram some years later they would not be able to maintain momentum although for a time they were the epitomy of tonal sciatica. These were the forerunners in the grey mist. Black hair began sprouting across the land.

In the wake of the originators came a more willowy breed. Ollie Wisdom, with his arguable sense of fun, opened The Batcave, using this as a launching pad for his glam-tat band, Specimen, a far cry from his tampon wearing days in The Unwanted, stars of the first Roxy Club album. (Lest we forget!) The Batcave, deservedly, became a much ridiculed establishment, that encouraged but finally debased any talent on show, for the gigs did little in the way of inspiring, as the dandies within gathered solely to preen damp feathers. Specimen, who were not to last long, landed a big record deal and themselves in a load of trouble.

Ollie reportedly started a new club and band later in America before returning, guitarist Jon Klein became a Banshee and Jonny Slut joined the adorably wild Diskord Datkord.

While the Batcave was lumbering on, less shallow minds sought refuge in Cloudy's The Tribe club, which coincided with the 'Positive Punk' phenomenon, a movement that nobody ever claimed existed in the first place and was mainly based around two whole bands! Minimalist? Sort of. The cabbalistic Blood And Roses, quite striking in their narcotic manner, and definite precursors for what has happened today, mixed a warmth and sensitivity, usually cast in sour shapes, with some debonair pop interiors. 'Love Under Will' was a demure enough début, followed some time afterwards by the marred pop *classic* 'Some Like It Hot', which would be perfect, hilarious though it may seem, for Patsy Kensit to cover. (In *what* is not for us to consider.) Our old pals Brigandage completed the deadly duo, spurred on by one Richard North of

Danse Society. Never before was so little achieved by so few, surprising so many! (Great band though.)

the *NME*, who would actually join the band on bass at one point, who wrote the cover story that never was. London Weekend Television, in a burst of sheer madness, cajoled Michael Moorcock into hosting a 'South Of Watford' documentary about it. A truly desperate effort.

The floodgates opened then, notably allowing Alien Sex Fiend through. One of today's most undervalued bands, yet totally unconcerned by such petty matters, they take emotional traumas and dead ends and decorate their walls with them. Their gigs are the total re-enactment of Hiroshima, and Uncle Nik Fiend, sneaking about in Alice Cooper's dressing gown may be an oddity of a 'singer' but he is also a living metaphor for the dangerously pulsating brain of today. They have crossed the world, under their own steam, as though the 'Living Dead' was their travelogue.

From then on you could count the 'Goth' bands on the fingers of one

battalion, and in truth it *became* ripe for knocking, what with Twisted Nerve and Seventh Seance and a whole *host* of bands who got it wrong. Only the recent improvement in vitality and ability, with continued audience support/involvement has made it the genre that the papers cannot afford to ignore, as they would prefer. Nobody can afford to alienate all their readers all of the time. Back in those lukewarm days, Action Pact, an incisive, frequently witty, punk band, drew upon lyricist Kim Igoe's observations for their naughty 'Gothic Party Time':
'There's gonna be a Gothic party,
Nosferatu's our host,
We're going to the Gothic party,
Crowley is the *most*,
Join me in the danse macabre,
Don't forget the witches garb,
When the guests are mingled in,
We'll discuss pre-war Berlin,
Ouija bored? Then come with me,
Through spiked railings you will see,
Edgar Allen,
Dorian Gray,
Decadent games we shall play.'

('Gothic Party Time',
Jungle Records.)

Shameful behaviour of course but peculiarly apt. Bandwagon terrorists such as Crown Of Thorns or Actifed might normally have been allowed access, had it not been for the sheer proliferation of bands, as well as some mightily impressive imports. America provided little of interest, since too many people shied away from what might almost be considered The Cramps' monopoly on the area. Goth, Shock, Horror? It's all rock'n'roll to them. Tex And The Horseheads had a singer with the occasional inverted crucifix, but they

Right: Action Pact. Seen posing on top of Gary Bushell.

Far right: Alien Sex Fiend. Sadly they never made it to 'T.O.T.P.'. And Steve Wright was absolutely aching to introduce them.

sounded post-autopsy half the time, the lamentably 'comic' 45 Grave, fronted by Dinah Cancer, were nice, but there was really only Christian Death. Did I say 'only'? Christian Death are the ultimate life is art, art is life brigade. To scoff at them is to wear a huge neon sign stating, 'I Am A Retard' above your head.

Europe, altogether more responsive, gave us Clair Obscur, Camp Sophisto, Les Provisoires, Strafe Fur Rebellion and the oddballs Belfegore, who lined themselves

up a nice deal, only for the singer to apparently run off with the advance! Pretty damn cool!

As you might expect the more enlightened coverage of the bands initially occurred in the fanzines of the day. These mainly involved *Kick* (produced by Richard North of the *NME*), *Vague* (by *ZigZag* stalwart Tom Vague, who meticulously dwelt upon every episode of Cult life), *Kill Your Pet Puppy* (one-legged Tony de la Fou, another *NME*

Right: The Cramps. A remarkable influence of American Goth bands of the late 80's, they also exert a similar hold over rock 'n' roll outfits. But where are they now? (Frankly my dears, we don't give a damn.)

Far right: Christian Death. Goth personified! Seen here going back to the womb, they are usually to be found rushing to their graves.

Richard North

Tom Vague

Tony de la Fou

Right: Crazyhead. Not Goth at all. Not Grebo at all. Just blurdy excellent!!

Over page: Gaye Bykers On Acid.

and *ZigZag* contributor), *Panache* (yours ever-so-truly), *Whippings* and *Apologies*, the main Northern title, and the ultra-dedicated *Artificial Life*, produced by Jake, a determined young man who even managed All About Eve at the start of their multifarious career. Behind these came the whippersnappers, *Grim Humour*, compiled by Rich and Andy, now committing aural atrocities with the group Playground, and *Day Of The Raygun Cometh*, an epic production from insatiable inebriate Louise Raygun. Wits have seldom been so sharp outside of the established press, which these days tends to pick up on such activists fairly swiftly and lure them on to the payrolls, promising life-enhancing interviews with Roger Whittaker.

Certain regions had little in the way of Goth activity. Maybe Scotland kept them buried but there wasn't the usual activity North of the border as might have been expected and even Ireland only managed Doomed Youth. Wales. . . well, that's Wales for you, while Yorkshire was positively overrun with the blighters! Southern Death Cult splitting somehow led to the formation of Getting The Fear which, after a troubled period at RCA yielded just one bumptious single, was whittled down further to become Into A Circle, a band more famous for its singer's pierced appendages than for anything noticeably musical. Gad, there was Cold Dance, Leitmotiv, Party Day and Ipso Facto, all deliciously pert in their own way but hardly Goth personified, but then that didn't matter any more. The Goth crowd liked them, which was another development. There was also, led by *Skeletal Family*, a litany of 'S' bands — Siii, Silent Scream, Second Coming and Salvation.

Down South you had The Veil, 3-D Scream, Cadaver Finesse, Sunglasses After Dark, all of them suitably chronic but impishly loveable. Bone Orchard, Exit Stance, Elephant Talk, The Possessed and Hysteria all did their bit for the coastal areas, straying as far West as possible and who can possibly forget Dormannu? Just as I thought. . .

Goth as we knew it had changed. It had gone! Almost, being replaced by bands who would try hard to shrug off the tag. New Model Army were hybrid rock, Rose Of Avalanche tried hard to convince people that they were American, or even that they were enjoyable, but it didn't really matter because judgement had started going out of the back door with the unwelcome visitors coming through the front. Even bands now, like Crazyhead or Gaye Bykers, and their inspiration, the wonderfully addled Bomb Party, have had to do battle with titles, generally referred to as 'Grebo'. Where will it end? Simon D, no relation to faded television professionals, once leader of The March Violets and now leader of the pack called Batfish Boys, sighs a terrifying sigh and says, ''Ripping off Led Zeppelin badly is the ultimate crime, and being *accused* of ripping off Led Zeppelin when you're not.''

So if people call him a Hippy?

''I'd probably bite their head off. The rebirth of the dirty rocker?'' he ponders thoughtfully. ''Before, in the sixties, acid was taken to try and 'find' yourself. Now it's taken to escape from yourself. Same thing with music. Whereas before, Led Zep might have been something amazing to be into, now it's like attempting to reverse our troubled times and escape.

''You can cross Hip Hop with Metal,'' Simon reasons, ''so you can cross Goth

with hippy which would be 'Gippy'; with metal, which'd make it 'Gimippy', and it just goes on and on! It seems everyone's looking for something to blend together and make their own cup of coffee but I think the main reason it's happening *is* because kids of that age haven't heard of that music and it's a new thing, but as regards all this imagery, what *do* people think they're doing? It's hideous!!!''

This Hippy and Grebo and outright dated Rock segment is surely dying. Simon Detroit would even lay money on it.

''And those happy little microbes with the strongest sense of melody will be left at the end. There's no way you can stop it until it falls apart which is, pessimism akimbo, what will happen and something else will come along.''

Which will be what?

''People playing bits of toast or something.''

Fresh impetus into the Gothy scene seems unlikely and from now on it will be startled follicles that greet you upon the boards, as the music veers towards excess, pure and unbridled. Should you care to sample these sirenic bulldozers you could do worse than Joan Of Arc Family, Rosegarden Funeral, B.C., Sleeping Dogs Wake, Bible For Dogs and Sins Of The Flesh. Doubtless between the time of writing this and you purchasing it another dozen will have sprung up, but I'm sure the end result will be pretty much the same as they hitch up their skirts, ruffle their codpieces and try and prop up the black economy.

We must bid them all a fondled farewell now, for it is time to take a well deserved look at the latest champions of this crusty territory, through the. . . *arched window.*

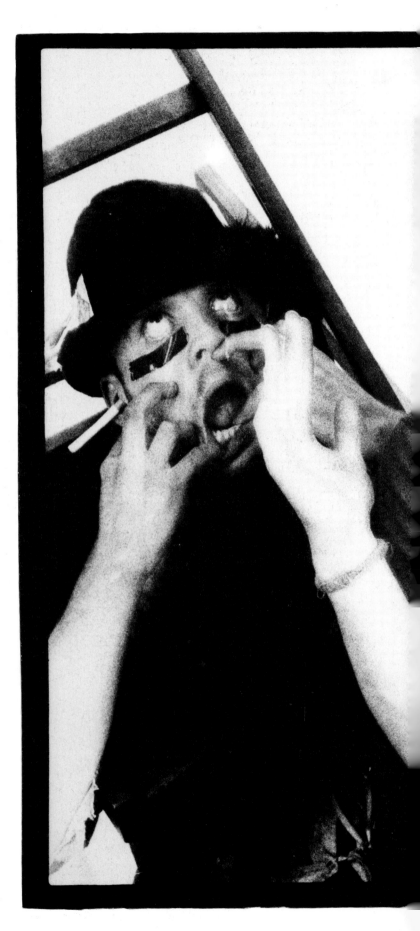

ALL ABOUT EVE

ALL BECAUSE THE LADY LOVES . . .

In that peculiarly brattish way we British have, there is a tendency to regard anyone who broaches the charts as suddenly becoming a senile delinquent, who turns rapidly from a normal, convivial, trivial person into a maliciously shallow-minded, unbearably smug egomaniac with a hall full of mirrors and a loft *buckling* under the weight of decapitated squirrels and half-digested choir boys. Normally of course this is quite true but there *are* exceptions to this far from golden rule and the politely absent-minded All About Eve, aghast at what they achieved in so short a time, when half way through their career they thought it was downhill all the way, are happily beyond reproach. Almost too nice for their own good, but hopeless at enacting a sneer, they could be engulfed at any minute by the big bad Business if it wasn't for a charming, totally natural stupidity that at times borders on the uncanny!

They have up their unbearably colourful sleeves certain songs which a typical elephantine band would give the full 'epic' treatment, which they can only sit back, staggered by, unable to do it anything but the finest justice. No pomp or circumcision, just sleepy, wistful, fluttering bullets which rarely kill but bring down the intended targets anyway, foaming in resignation at their wounds. Try as hard as you might, there is no ignoring *the charm*. To achieve such halcyon melodies when they often plummet into disused wells through misreading life's childishly simple reference points is just part and parcel of this weird operation. It has always been that way and when it stops happening by almost, and here's a word appropriate to them, *freakish* good fortune then the

All About Eve. Gothippyrockers? Or pop in a rare distillation of emotionally evocative esplanades? Possibly both.

chances are that they will have lost the truly magic spark. If that happens they could all follow their other predestined course — being the next Dr. Who assistants.

Their history is a balmy, convoluted one, easily worked out with a slide-rule, atlas and tea-leaves. Tim and Andy we shall ignore for the moment, imagining them, chums since their undercarriages dropped, preparing to join the windy Northern band, Aemotii Crii, who never actually made it on to vinyl, and we shall follow instead the course of Julianne Regan, forsaking her Midland bedroom, where she had hidden herself away with a collection of Japan records, as she hits London, determined to be . . . a music journalist! Remarkably enough she almost did it too, talking her way into writing a minuscule piece on Gene Loves Jezebel for *ZigZag*. I shan't embarrass her by reprinting any of it, apart from the opening line, 'At last, a welcome enema has been shoved up the weary backside of a stagnating scene'. At the same time she predicted that fellow Coventry soulmates 'I', a band who took to wearing monks' habits, would have a surprise Christmas hit in 1982, and blow me if they didn't! More disturbing was her frank admission that Wasted Youth had become an addiction. ('After a week I get withdrawal symptoms.') Somehow I don't think I should be telling you this, but isn't it fun? Further, apparently sensible, pieces appeared on Vane, The Passage and Modern English, then she was gone, joining the ranks of Gene Loves Jezebel on suppositories and bass.

"I can't even believe I was in it," she now claims. "I do feel they took me for a ride a bit. I was such a starry-eyed kid, thrilled to be in a band, to learn I could

Right: Manuela, ex-X-Mal (!), occupied the drumstool initially. Then she toddled off to have a baby.

Below: 'The Swarm'. Prior to All About Eve, Julianne and Manuela had plans to make Chris Club (Vague fanzine) the laughing stock of the nation. This line-up fortunately achieved nothing.

play an instrument and just *giving* all the time . . . they took all the time. There's no malice there because they did stick their necks out taking me on and I'm grateful for that.''

When this fell apart Julianne peered around her, taking stock, without a hint of shoplifting, falling in with Manuella Zwingmann who had just vacated the drumstool of X-Mal Deutschland. Together with a most unlikely choice, the fop-haired Chris Club of *Vague* fanzine, entirely untainted by musical talent, they considered something that would fill up their time and fill their minds with bravado. Tim Bricheno, having left Aemotii Crii, stumbled into view. Andy Cousin would do likewise, first stopping off to make a record with Pink And Black, 'Sometimes I Wish', featuring Rob Stroud (ex-Sex Gang, now Cosmic 666) and Michelle Yee-Chong (now Junior Manson Slags).

Operating briefly as The Swarm, with Tim firing off his guitar and some Ferguson chap on drums, the songs took shape, one of them being 'D For Desire' that would emerge as the début single in 1985 on their own Eden Records, clad in a 23 Envelope sleeve designed by Vaughan of that celebrated company. With James Richard Jackson on bass they managed to get through their lean cuisine, deflecting Cocteaus comparisons, *just*, with a sturdy energy and the great line, 'I cram my head with your sanity' on the B-side, 'Don't Follow Me (March Hare)'. Taped evidence of other songs, including 'This Isn't Heaven' show nicely rocketeering drums, as 'A Trembling Hand' quivered with strident squalls of wandering vocals, but they all outstay their welcome, usually rescued by neatly watchful guitar. Julianne's voice didn't sound anything

like it sounds today, rendered more through a funnel, her sponge-like awareness of what was going on around her restraining a natural flow.

Andy, bass held like a Napoleonic musket, jutting from the hip as though he wished to *invent* phallic imagery, joined them for a second single, an ethereal toast rack entitled 'In The Clouds', which should be eagerly sought out by collectors for the strikingly evocative flips of 'End Of The Day' and 'Love Leads Nowhere'. This time with a drummer called Matt Kemp they not only found their feet, but managed their finances

printing and apparently it was a very expensive print, so we thought we'd cut as many corners as possible on this one and exploit an under-five year old.''

Could the lyrics accurately be described as Hippy shit?

''Yes, I've got no defence for it,'' Julianne shuddered. ''That's *exactly* what it is. How embarrassing! I was very into God lyrics at the time and one day Tim said do you think you could get it together to write some *non*-God lyrics? When you look at the words it's a bit dodgy, because they're so dopey and naïve that somebody could really laugh

Pink and Black. Clockwise we find Andy Cousin, Michelle (now in Junior Manson Slags) and Rob Stroud (ex-Sex Gang, now Cosmic 666.) Short-lived poppettes.

'In The Clouds' was a 1986 release, as was their track 'Suppertime' on the ZigZag/Situation Two compilation album, 'Gunfire And Pianos'. They hadn't exactly shocked record companies into offering vast fortunes after seeing their nervously humming live shows, although Cherry Red proved to be in mischievous mood, calling the band in to make them an offer they could *all* too easily refuse.

"We didn't laugh," Julianne remembers, "because there was such disbelief."

Tim: "Oh God, it went really quiet! The big guy who runs it disappeared when it was time to mention money, sent his lackey in to break the news. Tried tarting it up with, 'We'll do a photo session, we'll get you on telly' but the bottom line was it was 750 quid."

Before something truly momentous happened to the band, as it would, they found paranoia as easy to embrace as the next band, worrying that their lack of personality onstage was putting people off, that 'Goth' was an albatross hung round their collective necks and an image, something frightfully different, *had* to be the answer. And maybe it was, although not what they originally had in mind, which was to wear white from head to foot and paint the instruments the same colour! No doubt the drum machine ("It's just like a servant," Louise Raygun learnt. "It doesn't merit a name") would have been slipped into a strategic and diplomatic pillowcase. Honestly, *some people*!

Julianne, as you will know by now, provided backing vocals on The Mission's albums and this alliance proved to be the turning point in the band's troubled past. As well as going on The Mission's tour as beaming support, Simon Hinkler and Wayne Hussey produced the third single and Mick Brown pounded the worried drums.

Things were looking up, ringlets permitting.

'Our Summer', which sadly didn't get close enough to crease the charts, let alone dent them, was a celebratory pop bash, complete with sublimely meaningless lyrics, but over on the *other* side . . . 'Lady Moonlight' and 'Shelter From The Rain'! Explanations were the order of the day when I tracked the band down to their hotel after taxing live work had taken its toll, and I was shocked. These people weren't just laid back, they were moonlighting (oops!) as spirit levels! Having escaped the 'Goth' tag, as planned, they were heading, totally unaware, for a potentially fatal weir.

They were quiet, their hair cascaded and, worst of all, Andy said 'man' a fair amount. As the table filled with glasses, opticians being such careless folk, the tale unfolded.

"It's not *that* bad," Tim rallied, stung by

Early Julianne live shot. The stage presentation involved the band filling their pants faster than the human nose could detect.

Hippy accusations and folding up a purely metaphorical teepee. ''It's just a joke isn't it?''

''NO!'' Julianne shrieked. ''It isn't.''

''No,'' Tim resisted, manfully. ''It *is*. 'Man' and 'baby', we don't *mean* that when we say it.''

Tough talk from a man I heard say, by way of an excuse-me, at the Marquee, ''I've just got to go and talk to this cat!''

''We've always been closet Hippies,'' Dr. Doolittle continued.

''It's the love vibration we've been talking about for so many years,'' laughed Julianne, as well she might.

Tim: ''Yeah!''

Andy: ''Man.''

Julianne: ''Oh dear!''

Oh dear? Make that oh dearie, *dearie* me!

''I don't think it's as obvious as you're making out,'' Tim whispered. ''We haven't worked it out but we realised we were playing up to the little audience. We did a massive showcase at the Clarendon and we thought we were going to be signed and it was all hanging on the gig and it was *bloody awful*.

Her left eye torn out by ravens, Julianne's mystical qualities only increased. Her voice began sending shivers down businessmen's longjohns.

Over page: Recovering from their infamous 'T.O.T.P.', where no sounds were heard at all, Andy cheers everyone up with his Dobbin The Pony routine.

71

We realised then . . . we were trying to be this hard, fast rock band with a girl singing over the top and it didn't work. It wasn't us. Then it started changing. We just decided to do exactly what we wanted to do, what we'd always wanted to do. We realised we were going wrong somewhere, so we stripped it right down, chucked out all the dirty guitars and started doing some really laid back ballads and stuff, building it from there and gradually introducing some faster songs and now we've got a good balance.

"It was a big risk, but we didn't really have that much to lose, did we?"

"At the moment," said Andy, feet in mouth, "we're just rocking. We're on a rocking vibe."

Julianne: "That was a really intelligent comment! We're into *songs* in a big way."

So, on all extents and purposes, Julianne's influence won through?

"Yeah, I suppose," Tim allowed, "because all I wanted to be was in some horribly glammy trash band when I came to London."

"Definitely," yodelled Julianne. "When I first met this man he was wearing a leopard skin collar. *And* bangles. Oh, how he's changed."

Tim (stonily): "How we've laughed about it. It's been nearly three years now and because we know each other very well it's just happened that way really, just everyone's been dead honest about how they feel. I don't think we were ever a *real* rock band. We wanted to be but we didn't really have what it really took to be A Rock Band. It's the sort of stuff we like to go and see and listen to but it wasn't what we knew we could do ourselves. I can't imagine us doing something like Ghost Dance."

I think they should take out insurance

There's no privacy when changing if they're on the road! Julianne makes the most of this lack of space. Tim, second from left, finds the non-existent toilet facilities more of a problem.

just to make sure!

The Mish of course turned out to be their saviours. All About Eve were swift to scotch comparisons.

"They're very hippy, trippy stuff," said Julianne, "but it's very rocky, whereas our stuff is on a more dreamy level. We were like this before they got to us."

And changed people after the tour, a rollercoaster ride into social misdemeanours.

"At Glasgow," Tim recalls, his bosoms heaving with pride, "it was 'YEAAHH!!!' for the first few numbers. I got my acoustic out and there was this sea of

flob towards it!"

"We were really upset," Julianne wept, "but apparently in Glasgow it's still a sign of appreciation."

"An extension of themselves'," Tim mutters, somewhat unconvinced. "So I went to bed a happy man that night."

And not just that night we suspect, being the foulmouthed readers that we are.

Following the release of 'Our Summer' came the record with the sleeve that actually cringed at its own title. 'Flowers In Our Hair'. Julianne, ever the gullible girl, had her own explanation.

"The point was, that the flower children got it wrong the first time round. So the song's about what it's supposed to be all about, without the trivia involved. It takes more than a joss-stick and a kaftan to be a sunchild my friend."

Their version of Rambo?

"I think it's too much of a tall order globally," Julianne piped up. "But for me personally, and my immediate friends . . . (she starts laughing uncontrollably) . . . I'm going for it!"

It? What does 'it' involve?

"I think it involves loving each other actually. We're on a big honesty trip. I'm afraid I feel like giving the kids a lot of love in there somewhere. How EMBARRASSING! I think people are suspicious, and rightly so, of anyone with a touch of Hippyness about them. A year ago Ian Astbury was Guru of Hippy and now he's Mister Heavy Metal! It's back to Peter, Paul And Mary. Rather than being Hippy it is 'Of The Past'. Rather than being terminally Curved Air we're more The Seekers. I think if we found ourselves disappearing up our own bottoms we'd all tell each other."

I can now reveal that they carried flashlights with them everywhere they went, *just in case*. Fat lot of good they did them. On the B-side of 'Flowers' you can find a version of Cliff's 'Devil Woman' that some people have rashly described as 'a cover'.

With all 'Goth' tags long since buried, but the Hippy accusations turning into a war crimes and witch hunt the band did little to clear their names. They re-released an improved 'In The Clouds', Julianne suddenly cast into a 'seductive' role in the video, cleavage perspiring, and there on the back was a nonentity, 'Calling Your Name' and a 'traditional arrangement' of 'She Moves Through The Fair' which was distinctly folk in the Clannad vein. No-one from centuries past was credited with this song, so if it was their own, and hadn't been released before how can it *be* 'traditionally' arranged? The poor Eves! Everyone was doing their best to love them and their wonderfully strong songs and all they could do was mystify the image further. 'Wild Hearted Woman' turned out to be a complete *cabbage* of a single. Coupled with the dreaded 'Appletree Man', traditionally arranged again, and a virtual sister song, 'Like Emily', even with the acquisition of the blissfully short-haired Mark Price on drums (ex-Nik Kershaw!) four anuses went *POP* and the stage was suddenly empty.

By the time they came round to releasing their album certain things had been shaken up, myself included for once. In isolation these could seem like syruppy songs, bracing with the big melodies but corny in deliverance, making perfect sense. Through their circumspect investigations and lolling livery, the Eves had come up with a smattering of shite, disruptive among the great songs, but overall a collection of diaphanous platinum. They had also got their shit together and knocked the mental blockages on the head, as they revealed in two *Melody Maker* interviews, with Chris Roberts and the Legendary Stud Brothers, as David Stubbs planned his infamous spoof, 'Julianne's Diaries': "But I must be ever so careful not to sneeze, for that will break the spell and we will fall down. Besides, a little elf will die", or how about, "Dearest Daddy has been a bit of a Mr Grumpy ever since last week when I drew all over the bathroom walls in pink crayon to cheer up the water

*Lordy! Britain's best!
Andy remembers he
has left his trousers
at home.*

babies that bathe there at night." ?

It's not fair is it? Not fair at all. Just hilarious, and Julianne takes the mocking of dream worlds very well, considering.

"It's the kind of thing you *can* switch on and off. You don't have to go through the gates of madness and get trapped in Fairyland and never come out. You can step in and out of that little world, and I enjoy being there. It's just that I used to live there and now it's an occasional holiday. I'm capable of depth *and* shallowness, and recently I've been on a shallow pleasure-seeking level. My last stint of shallow has lasted a long time. It *never* seeps into the music, that *is* deep. So I stress I'm going to get through a hermithood for a while soon and come out renewed. Tim always worries when I say this: he thinks I'm going to get the blanket out and read Nietzsche again."

Tim is a sensible fellow. Julianne made perceptive inter-band comments in the Raygun interview when she said, ". . . but Tim, he has this knack of bringing Andy and I back down to Earth, do you not Tim? You bring Andy — a human timebomb that boy — down from his pop star fantasies, and he brings me down from this artistic guru figure! He puts everything in perspective."

Tim: "The anchor man of the Eves."

Julianne: "*Exactly.*"

That album! That sherbet dab unfolding in Chris Roberts' longjohns, wasn't it a scary bruise at times, the way all the things you felt you wouldn't like, 'Wild Hearted Woman' and 'She Walks On For Bleedin' Hours' aside, suddenly rear up like Moby Dick, *sans* condom? Four singles (boo, hisssss), including their seventh, the timeless 'Every Angel', with an ever-so traditional 'Martha's Harbour' and 'Gypsy Dance', which *sums up* the

character of the band and Julianne's particular lyrical approach, which causes such confusion. Julianne can get herself hopelessly tangled up with rosily romanticised images, such as the gypsy campfire, and while that particular song is a quaint bucket of bilge, with the lyrics marginally less trite when written down — 'In a circle, in a ring, Gypsy dance, Gypsy sing, Gypsy dance to the tambourine, in fields of Green' — their naked honesty and freshness in the pop world of 'be a void and void those bowels', suggests that the woman who once wrote of enemas has become one! Carramba, metaphysical or what? Where, asked Chris Roberts, stumbling into a now still battlefield, had all the grief gone? Cleansed by the burning fire of love, Julianne had seen it peel off "like some really heavy molten grey eyelids", which proves a way with words if nothing else.

Best of all, there is included on the eponymously titled album a song called 'Never Promise Anyone Forever', which takes bitter recriminatory love angles, inside and out, rolls them into a ball and kicks it into your cornflakes. Julianne has come of age as a songwriter, and the band's music now matches the mood perfectly.

Quizzed by The Luminary Studebaker Brothel over the whole sorry Hippy episode, the band were equally sorry, and short on good excuses.

"A lot of it came out," Andy thought back, remembering the thrashings meted out by the press, "because of 'Flowers In Our Hair'."

Julianne: "Dumb move, wasn't it? I think we were asking for it really. The thing is, it wasn't totally to rip everybody off, I was dumb enough to actually believe in it for a brief period. And then I

realised I was being a prat and grew out of that little stage. It *was* just another stage.''

The world breathes a sigh of relief and disbelief.

''Sometimes we're a bit green you know,'' Julianne continued, ''always ready to believe something until proven wrong. We're just a bit daft and wet behind these ears sometimes. Gullible.''

So they have old folky imagery running riot through their tunes? So it's woodland glades rather than Everglades, so they're Good, rather than Bad, so they still believe in Father Christmas. Doesn't that somehow mean a lot? Don't you wish more bands maintained such a divinely simple faith in all around them? Don't you wish *somebody* would wipe the smile of that man from Wet Wet Wet?

For the final, perfect picture of what All About Eve are about, let me carve up some quotes from the Chris Roberts piece.

''We're always aware we often say, 'Oh, please, look, we're ordinary'. But we're not. We just keep it down. Like I'm sure John, Paul, George and Ringo had *depth*, but they assumed this armoured car of wackiness.

''I never thought it wouldn't happen. It wasn't ego, it was that I never let it cross my mind for fear of what on Earth I would think about then. Now things are a lot easier thanks to the good fairy Phonogram, but we'll never become complacent. We're staying firmly in obsessive perfectionist mode.''

All About Eve are utterly fabulous. A *farce* to be reckoned with.

The morning after! Another 'Sealed Knot' campaign reaches a soppy conclusion.

FIELDS OF THE NEPHILIM
A FISTFUL OF SQUALOR

And so, as the stains on your jeans simply *refuse* to . . . fade away, our time travel is almost at an end but for one more brief flip backwards through the ionosphere, to a small pub in Clerkenwell, East-*ish* London, where Nod Wright, diminutive Nephilim drummer, is making a complete *knob* of himself.

"I wanted to be a DJ," he announces, lips flecked with ale, "when I was really little."

"You still *are*!" explains bassist Tony Pettit, anxious to avoid anecdotal catastrophe.

"I made a disco once, I was *that* into it," Nod gibbers excitedly, "Y'know . . . fairy lights, off a Xmas tree? I whipped 'em off, stuck 'em on a Scalextric thing and stuck *them* on Subbuteo boxes covered in tin foil!"

"Last week, when we were off?" asks Carl McCoy, unleashing thunder from his throat.

"I used to go and do parties!!!"

I find it inconceivable that people don't like Fields Of The Nephilim, or at least *recognise* their achievements. Not only have they succeeded on a superfluous level – making the vicars of *Top Of The Pops* look so splendidly facile as they struggle with pronunciation – not only do they stick out like sore thumbs in a 'Sooty for Hire' sex scandal, but they have forced their presence to come through without one iota of the ideals being diluted. For too long ridiculed as foul Sisters clones, by people too feeble to even take the trouble to see them, they have worked their flour-coated arses off, with ceaseless touring, bringing botulistic mayhem to where it is needed. A unique course of events. *These* days.

The poisonous plebs who snort like hippos about their rise, many of them

profoundly miffed; doubly so because the *band* did it, nobody else, have to face facts.

The Nephilim had a goal, and they scored it. Couldn't be simpler. Always more resonant than the supposed victims of their 'crime', they took guitars and launched a sound at the audience which was resolutely devoid of the stench of archaeology, and in amongst the ground glass savagery, smoke, fried pain and Carl's gnarled vocals, there are moments of spellbinding beauty. Odd patterns, shapes pulled out of potentially nauseous tendrils, then tamed and re-shaped. Mean hombergs, that neutralise negativity. (Ooh, I say!)

Paul Wright, the shorter guitarist, sits, stunned by the news that The Nephilim – let's drop the 'Fields' bit, in case Gracie gets uppity – have clambered into the charts. As a man much troubled by spiders in my typewriter, I understand these feelings. Writers just stare. Where, they ask with deflated egotism, have they sprung from? Why haven't they gone away? *How much longer*? One might ask, as I frequently do, why don't these people ever learn? Push, Mr. Spencer (as expected), Lisa Tilston and myself have tried telling people, but the idiots know best. Until proof comes along. As it always does. That, I'm afraid, is History. And so is *this*.

Originally Tony Pettit, Gary Wisker, their one time keyboard/sax player, and the Wright brothers, passed the time in a band called Perfect Disaster from their native Stevenage area, which in turn became . . . wait for it . . . The Mission, a name they dropped later for some obscure reason. Carl McCoy, unstubbled, collided with their ideas, and suddenly the spectrum was green, with Mrs. Yates'

"Well, we haven't had a hat for quite a few pages . . ."

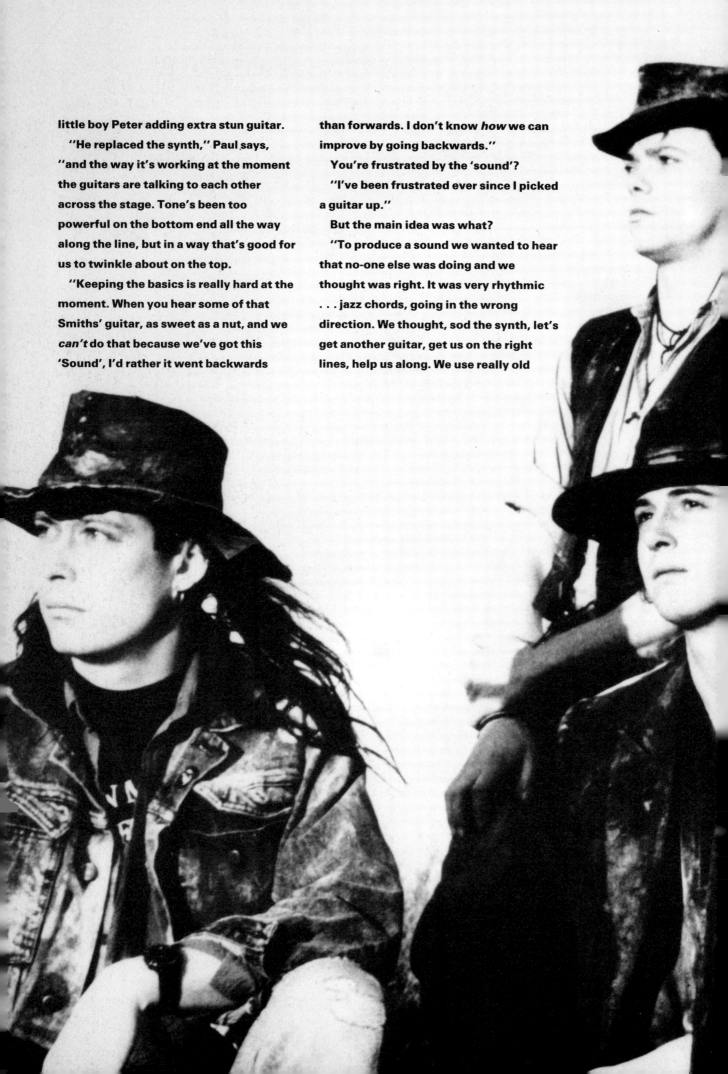

little boy Peter adding extra stun guitar.

"He replaced the synth," Paul says, "and the way it's working at the moment the guitars are talking to each other across the stage. Tone's been too powerful on the bottom end all the way along the line, but in a way that's good for us to twinkle about on the top.

"Keeping the basics is really hard at the moment. When you hear some of that Smiths' guitar, as sweet as a nut, and we *can't* do that because we've got this 'Sound', I'd rather it went backwards than forwards. I don't know *how* we can improve by going backwards."

You're frustrated by the 'sound'?

"I've been frustrated ever since I picked a guitar up."

But the main idea was what?

"To produce a sound we wanted to hear that no-one else was doing and we thought was right. It was very rhythmic . . . jazz chords, going in the wrong direction. We thought, sod the synth, let's get another guitar, get us on the right lines, help us along. We use really old

"Mel Brooks told us to wait right here. Something about a 're-make'?"

"Three cheers for Club 18-30 chaps. Best darned holiday we ever had!"

Carl, his voice honed with a daily gargle of bleach and creosote, likes to commune with nature. Even when he looks jolly silly.

gear, old guitars have got a certain thing. I don't know what the difference is but we like the old fashioned sounds. This technology thing frightens me. I can see myself becoming redundant! I can smell it coming, sampled and stuck on a deck!"

Never being slow in coming forward, The Nephs broached vinyl in November 1984 with the surprisingly, in retrospect, *skinny* four track 12-inch EP 'Burning The Fields', featuring the expected wash of weaving guitar, loping rhythms and gargled vocals, although decidedly polite. All the eerie and blustery hallmarks of their sound are there, as well as the first version of the lugubrious 'Laura'.

"That EP doesn't represent what we're playing right now," Paul says, stating the obvious. "It's a natural development. We haven't gone out of our way to write pop songs. I can't say The Mission have either. That's 'evolving'."

His eyes mist over.

"When you go to your first rehearsals and you realise what we've got going on here is an actual band and you can hear that *original* sound, the minute you find it, it's amazing. My brother's band is at that stage and I'd give my right arm to feel like that again. I'd like to regress in a certain way! I don't feel we've achieved everything we wanted . . . and that original feeling was *so* strong."

That initial line-up came when other bands they'd been 'sodding about' in folded; ("There's a lot of angry local bands around," Paul hoots), and the boys became united in their quest, united in their beleaguered instruments.

"Wonderfully, *gorgeously* out of tune guitars," Paul sighs. "The old smelly valve in the corner."

Bowel problems aside . . .

"It didn't gel really until Carl popped his

Over page: Bunfight at the OK Corral. Once again Stringfellows has refused them entrance.

head round the corner basically, although we had a lot of the first LP in our heads and when he came in it gelled because his ideas on top was just what we needed."

Was his voice the same as it is now?

"Miles more gruffer, but the gear we had at the time you couldn't hear him! He's still got a guttural voice but it's an honest one. I don't think he could sing any *other* way, besides he uses his voice as an instrument. You can even play it out of tune and it still fits together like one major chord, which is nice, all these out of order things going together, making certain chords and pitches when we're all flat out, that's another thing which has kept us together."

With their name, Biblical-based, on a race of giants, and their image, that has come along over the years, the time was obviously right for those early young Nephs to get going. They made one brief foray into the world of tape-bartering at record companies — "Carl and Tony did. They're a bit better looking, larger bulges in the underpants" — but nobody seemed too keen. Abstract almost smiled, the Majors laughed and the band pissed off. Creeping along to the 100 Club one night I caught the explosive whiff of the pre-Cowboy version, writing at the time, without the aid of stimulants, 'In this place a Stradivarius would sound like a clapped out old Renault. Nephilim may have two guitarists and a keyboard/sax maniac but you barely realise these duelling ingredients in the terrifyingly trim tumult, which crosses cultish (small 'c') borders, kicked relentlessly along by a powerful and sophisticated drummer.'

Sorry, there's more.

'It's their physical presence which strikes you most, rendering their vinyl potential peculiar, because *in* their

87

walking-statue way they look like a defeated Napoleonic regiment ready to desert, momentarily caught shuffling about. Great wind-harassed ghosts from an attic in the sky, their deviously stunted and sometimes addled, grumpy, warty, occasionally beautiful music shows them to be crappily named but frilly, frothy, dangerously daring purveyors of tip-top tantrums. (Phew!)'

Crappily named indeed! (*Indeed*.)

Situation two, gimlet-eyed and razor-eared leapt with fountain pens poised and the pickling 'Power' resulted, a single that promptly penetrated the indie charts. Around this time, as Paul Wright remembers, the image hardened. Now they all had *bugles* in their underpants.

"People wanted something to identify with, definitely, because they couldn't understand 'Power' from a Goth band, because we were labelled a Goth band; post-apocalyptic-bloody-underpant brigade. We're getting 'King Of The Goths' now. I'd rather be King Of The Goths than sods of them all. That (the image) was a variation on a theme on everything going on around us and we felt rather than glamorise ourselves . . . that's where the flour started coming in, we'd dress down, not deliberately to be anti-everything. We're scruffy bastards basically."

"The clothes are practical and comfortable," Carl rumbles in an interview for *House Of Dolls* with Alex Kadis. "You could wear them anywhere. I could never wear a suit, so that's what attracted me in the first place. It's something we've slipped into. But it's nice because some people do come and see us first because of our image but then they realise that the music is our real strength. The way *we* look at it is if it

sounds good enough to us then it should be good enough for other people who want to listen.''

Oh be quiet!

Confidence must be the key. The band have yet to receive a beating in public for their grotty garb.

''You go in there,'' Peter says, referring to a public house, where they like a foaming tankard of sarsaparilla, ''and they don't know *what* the fuck's going on. You never get any grief unless you're asking for it; going in as Doctor Hard. They're more interested than angry.''

So, the band toured with Gene Loves Jezebel, they toured with Zodiac and Flesh For Lulu and 'Preacher Man', a trickling, circular seven inch thing, *really* put a yeti among the piglets. With a magnificent dodgy mutant video, they had finally, firmly caught people's attention and 'Dawnrazor', the début album, and easily one of the strongest in years, slammed cynics up against the fence. With the chunky chintz of 'Vulcane' or 'Powerkill', the gurgling 'Dust', ravishment was on the cards. I do believe a little *Melody Maker* quote is in order.

'Disregard all prannyish comments about this band. They have constructed something quite magnificent in a dismal time, when everyone tends to ape things of indescribable putrescence. The Fields provide a valuable alternative to just about anything.

'Unlike hip-slop like Swans or Young Gods, *some* rattlesnakes wag their tails because they're pleased to see you.'

And when I asked for a picture to be printed with it? They *laughed*! C'est la wee-wee. The band felt fairly proud of the record, although Paul's language is a *disgrace.*

"Are you sure this is the service station Carl?"

"I thought at the time it hit the tit on the nipple."

'Emmerdale Farm' thought so too and played one of the songs as background pub music. 'Miami Vice' have since expressed interest. Life *is* strange. The band's rise continued with more touring, Reading Festival, the release of the sumptuous, vulpine 'Blue Water' and an ever increasing following, all while the press by and large ignored them.

"We've developed an immunity," Paul says. It just gives you an edge. If you haven't got that edge you can spot it. You can spot bands that are pretending or copying. I didn't think we were copying either and we used to get that *so* much! I'm not really sure what they want, but they won't get it if they don't ask the right questions. There isn't no mystical magic, all it is down to is having an initial idea to start with. You don't have to be a professor, all you've got to do is have a gut feeling and push it, otherwise you come out with a load of old shit."

What's the most formidable thing Fields Of The Nephilim possess?

"Carl. Definitely. He's the only bloke in the world I've never understood. Or possibly not wanted to. He's his own man. Why pry, why interfere? He's all right for me."

Do you ever wonder about his brain?

"Nah, that's his department. I've got me hands full with the music. If I could be busier than we are I'd do it. Spend more time playing and improving it and possibly being a good long-term band. Having the right people round you is important: without having to discuss it, having people who can just come up with initial ideas before me and actually be able to go over the top — the right key, the right frame of mind, the right speed . . .

before any words are spoken at all."

Probably the nearest the shy McCoy has yet come to explaining himself came in FSM, as explained to Lisa Tilston:

"Maybe I think along a different wavelength to most people. I can't see life as it is, just getting older and dying and that's the end. I see a lot further than that. I can believe anything could happen. I could accept going down the street and seeing a knight on horseback. I could even expect it. I feel I should *be* in the Middle Ages really . . . seriously. I think in a different time. I can't accept this world. London, all these people. I can't accept anything as it is."

I did enquire once why he never wrote love songs, considering he's such a romantic.

" 'Power' is about a poltergeist who keeps raping this woman. That's got a bit of love in it I suppose."

Maybe he thinks along different wavelengths to most people. Such as the crowd, one of the fiercely loyal bunches we discussed earlier.

"If I can get as close to *their* wavelength," Paul states, "without getting drunk and farting about . . . I'd like to obviously, otherwise I won't know what they're like. On the other hand we play to ourselves anyway, which is probably why they like us. We do play to ourselves, in the smoke. Tone can come over and I'm playing his bass and he's flicking my gear and they'll never notice. It's nice to have that freedom and they're the ones who give us it actually because you don't feel under pressure with them. I don't think they'll hate us for doing well, I think they'll be proud of us because they've made us what we are. They should be proud of themselves as well, because they're an event. Be fair, they're

very critical, they only go and see certain bands because they know they'll enjoy them. They've had enough of crap bands. Where *are* all the real bands? The real music? I don't know, it's almost like we've come to a pitiful stage.

"As soon as you stop thinking about the music, stop seriously debating what you're doing between the five of you, is the time you stop improving and then you've got to be *content* with what you've got and we ain't content, not with the articles, not with the music. I like what we've done and can't say any of it's bad but I think we've a hell of a lot more to offer than 'Goth band of the year'."

Acres of chart success?

"I don't think so. I think we'll have our foot in there for a little while. On the other hand . . . I could be completely right! Who knows the secrets of black magic, eh?"

Eh?

"Besides, who is this big geezer in the sky dictating who, what and why? There must *be* an authority you can have a go at. If it's gonna get worse let's try and get in there now, open the door for a few other bands, like The Mission and Sisters probably opened it for us, in their own way."

"I don't feel like we're their clones, driving up their arses, but I know that bands like that being around doesn't do us any harm at all, and that's the truth.

"There's different things to worry about. One of them's technology, which I'm *not* into. I get technofear at the sight

Nod, first on the left, still dreams of his youth. Not difficult considering that it hasn't ended yet. Unperturbed, Carl continues to crack ribticklers.

Over page: Fields Of The Nephilim. The rebirth of flour power. (That's enough crap jokes . . . Ed.)

93

of this Walkman, I really do! We're gonna be under pressure not to improvise so much any more, 'cos the pressure's there to *get it right* . . . you get bigger and there's more at stake. We can do it live every time.''

As the book starts, so it ends. Do you see yourself becoming another Cult?

''I can't see it happening to us. I worry about it, yeah, but my conscience is speaking to me at the moment half the time, saying is this right, is it part of the music, is it going to *affect* the music? 'Cos the music's the only thing I'm interested in. The rest of it can get stuffed.''

Inside all this evident confusion are you stunned by what's going on?

''The songs astonish me, I think, 'Well fuck me! *This* doesn't sound anything like what we normally do!' You go through different phases. I'd like to try a few things that we haven't done yet and I don't think *will* get the opportunity. Possibly there'll be an experimental thing coming up, just things we don't wanna put on the LP but are too good to waste.''

Nephilim have done it the hard way, the *only* way and they now stand, eyes shaded against the sun, having *eaten* the map, wondering *what on Earth* is going on. As long as they do what they do best — hanging up paintings from which the contents *spew* forth — they'll do all right.

''I hope so,'' Paul grunts. ''The next LP we've already written but there's still enough room for us to try new ideas out. Basically, I'd HATE for us to know what the one after this will sound like. I don't know *where* the next chapter is going to take us.''

Next chapter? Who said anything about *another* chapter?

This is the end!

THE END

(Told you so!)